SPIRIT OF CRICKET

Spirit of Cricket

Reflections on Play and Life

Mike Brearley

CONSTABLE

CONSTABLE

First published in Great Britain in 2020 by Constable

1 3 5 7 9 10 8 6 4 2

Copyright © Mike Brearley, 2020

The moral right of the author has been asserted.

A CIP catalogue record for this book
is available from the British Library.

ISBN: 978-1-47213-398-4 (hardback)
ISBN: 978-1-47213-397-7 (trade paperback)

Typeset in Electra by SX Composing DTP, Rayleigh, Essex
Printed and bound in Great Britain by Clays Ltd, Elcograf S.p.A

Papers used by Constable are from well-managed forests
and other responsible sources.

Constable
An imprint of
Little, Brown Book Group
Carmelite House
50 Victoria Embankment
London EC4Y 0DZ

An Hachette UK Company
www.hachette.co.uk

www.littlebrown.co.uk

To Luka, Alia, Maia and Lila

'Although I have supported Somerset . . . since 1948, I'm afraid I did not enjoy the Gillette Cup Final very much . . . Can you imagine Napoleon addressing his troops just before Waterloo? "Remember chaps it's only a battle. Fight hard but fight fair. And the important thing is – I want everyone to enjoy himself. May the best team win."'

John Cleese, Somerset supporter, about the
1979 Gillette Cup Final

CONTENTS

YOU'RE NOT THE ONLY PEBBLE
ON THE BEACH

'Cricket was a way of life, near to godliness'
Bob Platt, ex-Yorkshire cricketer

I remember an end-of-term game for the school against the staff when I was fifteen or sixteen. I was keeping wicket. Their number eleven was an American exchange teacher, whose name comes back to me out of the blue or the blur – Mr Tillinghast. It turned out that Mr Tillinghast, a baseball fan, thought you had to run after two strikes. Having managed to hit his third ball, he hared off towards what was for him first base, joining his batting partner at the far end. The ball was thrown gently in to me. I took off the bails.

It is probably shame that brings back this event, and this name, to me. Shame registers the fact that I went against cricket's spirit, against common sense and generosity. Narrow correctness prevailed. I can put it down partly to immaturity. At least I took the bails off sheepishly.

Sometime later, when I first heard the phrase the 'spirit of cricket', I was suspicious of it, on two counts: first that it was vague; second that it could easily be pronounced from above, patronisingly, with absolute conviction of correctness. I felt it had been enlisted by snobbery.

But I've come to see that this is a distortion of the reality. In fact, all cricket people have their codes, lived out in their own individual and

1

group ways. Values are expressed bottom-up, usually without highly articulated rationalisations or awareness. Like other forms of life, cricket is the outcome of an informal social contract. It is a practice held together and supported by a set of mostly tacit agreements, all part of our legacy from past generations.

Like parental support and provision, its spirit is there in the background. Someone else looks after all that while we, as children and players, focus on playing the game itself.

Each April, we would lovingly massage our bats with linseed oil. Our excitement and anxiety focused on performance – can I continue where I left off last September? Will our team win any matches? 'Spirit' obtrudes consciously only when, as when rain stops play, a contentious issue gives us pause.

Conveyed in the varied voices and attitudes, there is a wisdom in crowds as well as the potential for barbarism. Values, many of them shared, run through cricket in all its incarnations – in parks, back streets, village greens, stadiums. The maidans of Bombay, which produced Sunil Gavaskar, Sachin Tendulkar and many others, await their chronicler.

The spirit of cricket empowers the game from grass roots up. As Brian Close put it (about coming into the Yorkshire side as a eighteen-year-old in 1949): 'The professionals' attitude was absolutely first-class at the time. If any of your own side tried to cheat, like hit the ball and not walk, your own players would set about them. There was such a high moral standard in the game.'

As with many moral precepts, fundamental maxims such as 'play according to the spirit of cricket' are not owned by any one group.

Even in religious contexts, advice or guidance ('Love your neighbour as yourself') need not be delivered *ex cathedra*. These maxims are best thought of as reminders of general orientations and attitudes in which notions such as fair play, respect, consideration and balance already predominate. Most professional cricketers of my acquaintance (myself included, until writing this book) have never sat down and read the Laws through. We knew most of them on our pulses. And we all have our unarticulated convictions and ways of going about things, on and off the field. We take much for granted, until we're shocked by some action or attitude of others or ourselves. Then the debate goes on in argument and discussions between people, and in the privacy of a person's soul, as much as from the archbishop's throne or the papal pulpit.

The most striking affirmative statement I know of the value of sport comes from Albert Camus: 'All that I know most surely about morality and the obligations of men, I owe to football.'

I don't, however, share Camus's experience that these values were conveyed and learned *specifically* in the area of sport. When I think of my sense of how things were for me, the childhood quality that was the most common locus for moral criticism was 'selfishness' or 'self-centredness'. 'You're not the only pebble on the beach,' my father would say. Boasting, too, was quickly put down. On the other hand, it was also a plain fact that we shouldn't undervalue ourselves. False modesty, or self-effacement, was not admirable.

Perhaps selfishness in cricket (especially) was more flagrant, more public, than it often was within the domestic sphere. I recall my father's impatience with me for blocking an off-spinner before at last hitting him over the top. More privately, feeling miffed that one had to retire on reaching 25 in practice games, I remember considering deliberately slowing down in order to be allowed longer at the crease.

But running out Mr Tillinghast was a failing of immaturity in general, rather than a cricketing matter in particular. I always knew, from cricket and from life, that it was a bad thing to be selfish, though of course that didn't mean I never was.

Now, having written the book, I acknowledge more than before the importance of many of cricket's traditions and values. Along with inevitable prejudices and snobberies, they have played their part in

3

encouraging people from many backgrounds to expect and internalise fair play without loss of wholeheartedness and passion. Phrases such as 'It's not cricket', common parlance to describe dishonourable behaviour in all walks of life, do often have a solid basis in the game itself. The spirit of cricket can be harnessed to worthy ends rather than to jingoism or superiority.

Everyone has their national myths, and one English myth finds a home in cricket.

I write this in June 2020, as in the UK we appear to have surmounted the peak of infections with the global phenomenon of Covid-19. This has been a horrible and indeed terrifying experience for many people; it provokes anxiety in us all. But no doubt some good may come of it.

We are faced with an enforced pause from the rush and routine of life. One of the many activities that we are all deprived of is sport. We face the prospect of a season with limited cricket. We have an unnatural break. Do we have the wit and wisdom to use this gap creatively? Might we – once the immediate crisis is over too – find time to consider the way we live our lives, including the spirit of something many of us love, namely cricket?

Through sport, as in religion, theatre, art or psychoanalysis, we offer ourselves timeouts from the necessary effort of making our livings and keeping the show on the road. With the current catastrophe of coronavirus, we have no idea what the dimensions of this enforced break from so much of what we considered to be normal life will be, nor how or when it will end. But what we do know is that nothing will be the same again, not at least for quite a time. Our larger cultural, societal and personal values may change for better or for worse. We can explore this issue on the large or the small scale. We may come out of it with a more selfish or a more unselfish orientation.

It may also permit questioning. Reflecting about the spirit, bringing reason to bear, may change our priorities. It may even reduce our tendency to fritter away our precious time. Reflection may lead to changes of opinion in cricket too, as mine has been changed over Mankading. We may come to see how a long-held attitude leads to rigidity, unfairness, even to injustice. Sometimes what we learn is that there is no single answer. There may be two or more sensible, reasonable answers, as there are for example (as I, unlike Close, see it) to the cricket issue of 'walking'.

The value of questioning applies also within the self. We may be better off if we can accommodate apparently contradictory attitudes or points of view, rather than offloading unwelcome beliefs and thus stereotyping others with qualities from ourselves, contributing to unnecessary schisms and antagonisms. Giving houseroom to our ambivalence is part of our human complexity; even in some ways of our human excellence.

I like the notion of challenging in the interests of truth, rather than accepting blindly in the interests of deference. I enjoyed learning one theory about the name 'Israel' for the homeland of the Jews: that it refers (by its etymology) to the Jewish tendency to wrestle with God, to argue things out, based as it is on the new name ('Israel') given to Jacob after he wrestled through the night with an angel, a messenger from God. In Hebrew, 'Israel' contains within it this notion – it is as if Jews announce: 'We are a people who argue with God – we don't accept things at face value, without struggle.' (I am unsurprised to learn that this etymology is itself disputed; another version is: 'May God show his strength.')

I like too the disputatiousness of the Talmud, the text that is a primary source of Jewish law and attitudes, in which commentaries on religious ideas have become part of the text itself. One corollary of this is the idea of a supreme authority that is not only omnipotent and demanding of obedience – a 'jealous God' – but one who will argue with his people and allow them to struggle with him on matters of truth and value. This may be one element in God's strength.

5

Jonathan Rosen writes that chaos may represent 'a divine fecundity', and a divine permission for wrangling. It is striking to me that the Talmud is a centrepiece of Jewish cultural and intellectual life.

Spirit of Cricket is not, or not obviously, a self-help book. It is not a manual. Nor is comparing it to the Talmud – a sort of treasure house of being wrong-footed – the most contemporary recommendation. And yes, I know, not every digression is a bonus. Cut to the chase, you may say.

But this is what it is.

This book is of course about cricket; but it also, I hope, has a broader relevance for much more.

1

SHARP PRACTICES

'If you want to call it anything, just say the batsman was "Browned", not "Mankaded".'

Sunil Gavaskar

Vinoo Mankad was one of India's finest cricketers. In 1952, he took 12 wickets in India's first-ever victory over England, at Madras, and later in the same year, at Lord's, after taking 5 wickets in England's first innings, scored 184 in India's second. Until one Ian Botham broke the record, he took 100 wickets and scored 1,000 runs in fewer Test matches than anyone else.

But many today know him only for one thing, and that's regarded as disreputable.

Twice during India's tour of Australia in 1947–8, he ran out batsman Bill Brown when the latter backed up too soon, leaving his crease before the ball was bowled. The first occurrence was when the Indians played an Australian XI. Mankad warned Brown, but when the non-striker again left his crease early, he ran him out. In the Second Test, again in Sydney, he dismissed him in the same way. Apparently, Brown was well out of his ground when the bails were removed.

This kind of dismissal has since been called 'Mankading'. It has been widely regarded as unsportsmanlike.

Don Bradman, Australia's captain in that Test match, defended the bowler, writing:

> For the life of me I can't understand why the press questioned this sportsmanship. The Laws of Cricket make it quite clear that the non-striker must keep within his ground until the ball has been delivered. By backing up too far or too early, the non-striker is obviously gaining an unfair advantage.

Seventy years on, in 2017, Sunil Gavaskar agreed with Bradman, suggesting that his fellow countryman had been unfairly criminalised: 'If you want to call it anything, just say the batsman was "Browned", not "Mankaded"'.

And the batsman himself said: 'I deserved it.'

Nevertheless, most cricketers and followers down the years have joined the chorus of disapproval. Actions that are felt to go against the spirit of cricket are not always illegal; many are, but others, though technically within the Laws, are objected to on grounds of ethics, of bad moral taste. Mankading is a case in point; cricket players and public across the board have agreed that it is unsporting. At every level, reactions have been vitriolic and self-righteous. Whatever the Laws said, we *knew* it was wrong. Or thought we knew!

In the last few years, opinions have shifted. In 2014, I watched England play Sri Lanka at Lord's in the fourth One-Day International of the series. Chasing a total of 300, England were 111 for 5 when Jos Buttler joined Ravi Bopara. The pair added 133 in 16 overs. During 10 of those overs, they scored 22 twos; many of them from hits against slower bowlers down the ground, to long off or long on. It became clear to me, sitting in the Press Box above the sightscreen, that the non-striker, who was likely to be running to the danger end for the second run, was starting early from the bowler's crease. I wouldn't want to call it cheating, but it was enthusiastic stealing a march. It looked as though this might make a difference to the result of the match. Earlier that day, Sri Lanka won by 7 runs, despite Buttler's magnificent 121.

Kumar Sangakkara, who'd scored a brilliant and assured century earlier in the day, told me later that the Sri Lanka captain had complained to the umpires about the lack of any proactive measures by them to stop this premature backing-up.

The final match of the series, which was level at 2–2, took place a few days after the Lord's match, at Edgbaston. Once again Buttler was batting; again, off-spinner Sachithra Senanayake was bowling. Twice Senanayake warned Buttler and, an over later, ran him out. England were dismissed for 219, and Sri Lanka won the match by 6 wickets.

The bowler, a young player doing what he was given licence to do by his captain and senior players, not to mention by the Laws of the game, was booed by the crowd.

We discussed the issue at the MCC (Marylebone Cricket Club) World Cricket Committee in the same summer. This committee is a think-tank on international cricket. The members are almost all ex-international players, from most of the main cricket-playing countries, and from cricketing generations all the way from dinosaurs whom I played with and against to current players. To my surprise, sympathy was almost exclusively with the fielding side in this scenario.

Either the batsman *was* stealing a march (note the term 'stealing'), or he was being dozy, people commented. As a result of the much increased use of cameras in decision-making, if a delivery that bowled a batsman neck and crop has been discovered afterwards (by TV footage) to have been a no-ball by so little as a fraction of an inch, the batsman will be recalled. No one will suggest that the bowler should be let off with a warning, nor will he win sympathy from team-mates or spectators. Doziness in sport is not generally rewarded by indulgent sympathy. Indeed, I would say that sport is as much

9

a matter of keeping your wits about you as of being exceptionally moral.

Moreover, now that fitness has become a key feature in the game, especially in limited-overs cricket, the inches gained by quick running, or lost to quick fielding, are often crucial. Several ex-players, especially bowlers, see the hoo-ha about Mankading as a nice illustration of the fact that it's always been a batsman's game – the benefit of the umpire's doubt goes to batsmen; in One-Day cricket bowlers are restricted in the number of overs they can bowl (batsmen have no such restrictions); and it's more often than not batsmen who get the juiciest sponsorships and, ultimately, knighthoods.

One member of that committee, ex-Australia Test cricketer Rod Marsh, goes so far as to suggest that no runs should be scored from any delivery if the non-striker leaves his crease early.

I too had changed my mind. I was no longer inclined to view Senanayake's action as unethical or against the spirit of cricket.

However, cases vary. Not everything fits into the same box. Five years afterwards, Buttler was again run out while backing up, this time in an Indian Premier League match. The bowler was Indian off-spinner Ravi Ashwin. This dismissal aroused different responses. There was no warning. And it seemed that before taking the bails off, Ashwin paused briefly with his hand near the stumps, waiting for Buttler's bat to be dragged over the line. It's arguable, too, that the decision was incorrect, since Law 41.16.1 states that: 'If the non-striker is out of his/her ground at any time from the moment the ball comes into play until the *instant when the bowler would normally have been expected to release the ball*, the non-striker is liable to be run out.' Owing to the delay, Buttler's leaving the crease seemed to take place after he would reasonably have expected the ball to have been released – though ICC and MCC's guidance to umpires apparently defined the 'moment' as 'the highest point in the bowler's action', a definition by which Buttler was correctly judged 'out'.

This second case is akin to entrapment, the kind of scenario when someone is lured into a misdemeanour and then punished for it – as with the newspaper sting that caught out three Pakistan players in 2010. The bowler's delay in breaking the stumps is a kind of invitation to the batsman to leave before the ball is actually bowled.

Along with many others, I felt that Ashwin's action was indeed too cunning, a bit shabby. But it's clear to me that the primary obligation is on the non-striker. It is his responsibility to wait until he sees the ball leave the bowler's hand.

As for Buttler, I'm reminded of Oscar Wilde's line: 'To lose one parent may be regarded as a misfortune; to lose both looks like carelessness.'

* * *

The condemnation of running a non-striker out when backing up too soon, and the more recent reversal of moral stance on this issue, were based not on (il)legality, but on what is or is felt to be sportsmanlike, what falls within the rubric of the spirit of cricket. For most of my lifetime, it was, in my experience, a matter of commonly-held assumption that Mankading was sharp practice, legal maybe, but obnoxious. Perhaps there was something subliminally racist in this view: named after an Indian, the action was felt to be un-Christian. Recently it has come to be seen through a different lens.

The sandpaper case, by contrast, concerned actions that were plainly against the Laws of the game. But matters did not stop there. The event exploded into notoriety, engaging the attention of people far beyond cricket. It raised issues to do with the orientation and general attitude of the Australian team, even of its organisation's culture. *Wisden Cricketers' Almanack* called it a 'farrago'. Many words have been written on the story, including by me in *On Cricket*. Here I will give the facts of the case as briefly as I can and speak about some of the implications. Why were so many people excited by it? Why were those convicted of being in on the plan punished so much more severely by their own Board? Did its occurrence say anything about the zeitgeist, about the spirit of the age?

In 2018, Australia toured South Africa, playing four Test matches. During the first two, there had been rancour between the teams. Indeed, at that Second Test the umpires and match referee had already spoken informally to broadcasters, asking if cameramen had noticed anything suspicious in what happened to the ball on its way back to the bowler. Perhaps in response to such suspicion, David Warner, Australia's vice-captain, who had been the person the team threw the ball to for polishing between deliveries before tossing it back to the bowler, had handed these responsibilities over to the young opener, Cameron Bancroft, for the Third Test at Cape Town.

Matt West/BPI/Shutterstock

On the afternoon of the third day, when Australia were up against it in the field, Bancroft was picked up by TV cameras surreptitiously putting a piece of what looked like yellow tape down the front of his trousers. He was caught not with his trousers down exactly, but with something down his trousers. Soon, and more to the point, camera sequences were discovered of him 'holding the ball in his left hand, scrubbing his cupped right palm and fingers over the leather as though battling an unforgiving doorknob. You could see the pressure he was applying by the white flush of his knuckles', as Geoff Lemon, who wrote an excellent book on the story, put it. He was, in other words, doing an energetic job of 'changing the condition of the ball'.

As people around the dressing rooms and media area became aware that incriminating images were about to be shown on the big viewing screens at Newlands, Darren Lehmann, Australia's coach, sent the twelfth man onto the ground to warn Bancroft. That was when Bancroft ('like any kid caught shoplifting a Milky Way', Gideon Haigh wrote) shoved the evidence down his pants.

It turned out that the yellow stuff was sandpaper, used to damage one side of the ball, roughing it up in an attempt to make the ball 'reverse' swing.

This skill was developed in the 1970s and beyond by pace bowlers in Pakistan, first Sarfraz Nawaz, then Imran Khan, Wasim Akram and Waqar Younis. Reverse swing is usually possible only when the ball gets older. Whereas with orthodox, newer-ball swing, holding the ball with its shiny side away from his thumb enables the right-arm bowler to swing it away towards the slips; with reverse swing, holding it thus makes the ball likely to swing the other way, in from the off. It has since become a regular tool of the trade for many fast bowlers, enhancing the interest and attacking nature of the game.

Law 41.3.2 states that it is forbidden for a player to 'take any action which changes the condition of the ball'. There are exceptions to this prohibition. It *is* (or was until coronavirus stepped in) legal to use sweat or saliva on the ball, an application which may help shine one side. Sweat may also be used to make the other side of the ball weightier. It has also been within legality to throw the ball in from the deep on the bounce, especially on dry and abrasive grounds, to make the rough side of the ball further worn and pitted.

Over the years there have been allegations and rumours in relation to reverse swing that fielding sides have used tools to accelerate the process – knives, scissors, sharp edges on opened Coke cans. Sandpaper obviously falls into this category, and the hiding of the offending material makes plain that this was perfectly well known to the participants at Cape Town, as to everyone in the game, then and now.

However, the long history of ball-tampering predates by decades this innovation. It never used to be seen as a serious offence. People have used their fingernails to raise the edges of the seam, to make deviation off the pitch more likely, rubbed dirt on the ball, and added sun-creams or other 'artificial' agents to get a better shine. For reverse swing, another ploy has been to raise the quarter-seam, the small join running counter to the main seam. In English cricket, umpires, many of whom had been bowlers in their playing days, did little to stop such actions. Umpires and players alike tended to view at least the less blatant practices as par for the course. Don't go too far, the unspoken message went, but don't get caught.

Reverse swing had been a decisive factor in previous series between South Africa and Australia. And early in the 2018 tour, Lehmann was relaxed. 'Obviously, there are techniques used by both sides to get the ball reversing. I have no problem with it. Simple.' (Or not so simple: the pot won't bother to call the kettle 'burnt-arse'.)

In 1994, during a Test match at Lord's that also, as it happened, involved South Africa, England captain Mike Atherton was fined £2,000 for having soil in his pocket. He said it was to dry his hands and to take moisture off the ball. If he had used the soil on the ball it would therefore have been a matter of maintaining the condition of the ball, not changing it – as innocent as having a cloth to hand to keep the ball dry – something explicitly permitted in the Laws, provided that the cloth had been supplied by the umpire. He was not banned.

In 1977, there was a flurry of protest in India against MCC's team, of which I was vice-captain. After the Third Test at Madras, now called Chennai, India's captain Bishan Bedi accused John Lever and Tony Greig (the captain) of cheating, alleging that Lever used Vaseline to change the condition of the ball. In fact, what had happened was that he and Bob Willis asked physiotherapist Bernard Thomas for a method to keep the sweat out of their eyes when bowling. Both had long hair, which didn't help. Thomas made headbands from gauze impregnated with Vaseline, to be taped to their foreheads to stop the passage of sweat. Lever, who had taken ten wickets in the First Test at Delhi, had swung the ball there at least as much as in Madras, without headband or Vaseline. Willis had not swung a ball in either place. When the headband became cumbersome, Lever put it down behind the stumps without any attempt to hide it. Though it was of course possible that traces of the Vaseline had got onto the ball via his habit of using his sweat to polish the ball, this had neither been his intention nor had it (as far as anyone knew) affected the ball or the bowler's ability to swing it. He now wishes he had never asked Thomas for assistance.

As vice-captain, I was part of the leadership group, but I don't remember any conversations about it or its legality. Perhaps this was naïve of us. Certainly, it would have been better to have cleared the use of these bandages with the umpires from the beginning. But I'm sure there was no devious intention.

Ball-tampering has never been regarded as a serious crime by international authorities either. In the 2018 ICC Code of Conduct, which gives guidance about disciplinary charges and hearings, there were four levels of disciplinary charge; that for breaking this provision was either a Level 1 charge, along with throwing one's bat on the floor when given out or uttering an expletive on the field, or a Level 2 charge, as when someone directs personal abusive comments at an opponent (the accusation against Shannon Gabriel for his abuse of Joe Root, which I describe later). Levels 3 and 4 concerned more serious matters, such as racist abuse or deliberate physical contact.

At the disciplinary hearing in Cape Town held by the match referee that evening, the sandpaper incident seemed to have been a regular sort of case of tampering with the ball. The players concerned were punished according to the usual tariffs for such offences. It was admitted that the behaviour on the field carried out by the junior player had been a 'decision of the leadership group', with the full knowledge of Australia's captain, Steve Smith. As a result, Smith was charged at Level 2 for the decision, which 'risked causing serious damage to the integrity of the match and was contrary to the spirit of the game'. He was given four demerit points, entailing a one-Test ban, while Bancroft, who admitted a Level 2 charge related to 'changing the condition of the ball', received a fine and three demerit points (no ban). (Demerit points are a set of bad marks that can entail or build up over time to a ban. Once the ban has been imposed, the points remain applicable for a further two years.) Warner, later discovered to have been pivotal to the plan, had not yet been implicated.

This was bad enough for those involved and for the whole team, but it was nothing compared with what followed. What started as not much more than a spark blew up into a raging bush fire. Outrage mounted, above all in Australia itself. The players had betrayed the country. Prime minister Malcolm Turnbull, interviewed on television, announced: 'To the whole nation, who hold those who wear the Baggy Green up on a pedestal – about as high as you can get in Australia – this is a shocking disappointment. How can our team be engaged in cheating like this? It beggars belief.' The episode earned a place on the ten o'clock news in the UK, where a certain *schadenfreude* became apparent. As ICC (International Cricket Council) CEO David Richardson said, cricketers beyond Australia needed to take a look at themselves, a requirement that went beyond the players to administrators.

Soon emissaries from Cricket Australia were in Cape Town. Smith, Warner and Bancroft were interviewed and soon banned from all cricket – the first two for a year, Bancroft for nine months. Smith would not be considered for the captaincy for at least two years; Warner would never be given a leadership role within the team. They were sent back home, in disgrace, on separate planes, and were 'tried' on television. All shed tears, of shame and guilt, as did Lehmann, who resigned soon after. Smith admitted that what they did went against the spirit of cricket. Questions were raised about the sincerity or otherwise of Warner's tears, and about his refusal to discuss anything beyond his repeated mantra of his own culpability. I thought he was manfully sticking to his brief, clinging to the vestiges of self-respect by holding on to the Australian concept of 'mateship' – don't ditch your mates. For it was impossible to imagine that other members of the team did not know about the ball tampering, especially the bowlers, for whom the state of the ball is one of the most crucial elements in their armoury.

Once the world at large had observed the players' confessions, humiliation and shame, the impetus of the outrage declined. One could not watch these interviews without feeling sympathy for these young men, brought up in an atmosphere that made winning the main aim in playing for Australia. They were in part propagators, in part victims of this kind of imperative.

Indeed, almost all those running Cricket Australia succumbed to pressure within a few months, leaving or being sacked. I think this was probably right. They, as well as members of the media, should share some of the blame. Too many were complicit in the ruthless stance. In politics, racism and other hate crimes offer a parallel. Those who by their words express xenophobia and prejudice, and who turn a blind eye to the extreme behaviours of some of their followers, as CA had done over the years with some of their players, must take some responsibility if they give implicit encouragement to individuals who carry out in action attitudes that had previously been insinuated in words. Remember the alleged words of Henry II: 'Who will rid me of this turbulent priest?' The knights took the hint, and soon Thomas à Beckett lay dying in Canterbury Cathedral.

So what fanned this forest fire? On the face of it, the three had not done anything terrible. Clearly the reasons lay beyond the simple act of altering the condition of the ball.

One element was precisely the fact that the misbehaviour occurred within sport, rather than in some more obviously significant area in a person's life. As Indian cricket writer Suresh Menon writes, 'Had Bill Clinton cheated on the golf course, there would have been no redemption'. Moreover, it is, Menon suggests, because sport is meaningless that it has to be rescued through higher morality. 'In a fantasy world [of sport] we should aim for perfection.'

More important, I think, was the emerging fact that the Australian public were already cynical towards and disillusioned by their national cricket team. Moments after the news first broke, my friend Kate Fitzpatrick emailed me that she had been: 'disenchanted and disheartened by Australian cricket for a long time. But the moronically stupid, entitled, childish, ill-bred, cowardly performance hammered the lid down for me . . . All the bully boys have to go.' She made the excellent further point that it was 'the only thing they could think of in the face of a flogging'.

To be more precise: I think there were several separate and specific reasons for the severity of the bans CA imposed. First there was the fact that it was not spontaneous, but planned, calculated. Second there was the fact that the actual deed was left in the hands of the junior player (Bancroft). Third, and most important, this was the straw on the camel's back. There had been a constant drip-drip of stories of crude antagonisms and streaks of nastiness, and this had gone on through several recent series, against India and England as well as South Africa. Fourth the players' reactions to being caught were, for a while, inadequate and dishonest.

As Kate said, all this supports the idea of a childish sense of entitlement. She also hit the nail on the head in her comment about this being the only resort they had to prospective defeat, especially after losing the previous Test in Port Elizabeth. The more one's well-being is reduced to 'tread on them or they'll tread on you', or 'dog eats dog', the more failing feels like humiliation, and the more one is likely to grab at any means of getting back on top (for example, by cheating). We are liable to slip into a gang warfare mentality.

Indeed, this view was put forward with sharp clarity by Tom Derose and Ivan Ward from the Freud Museum in London. They suggested that, at the deepest level, the humiliation was that of castration. The young men, feeling weak and impotent on the field, rebelled against the father and his rules. Tampering with the ball, they tried to change its qualities, to turn it into a powerful phallus, so that, instead of helplessness in the face of South Africa's dominance, they could become instantly potent. Caught in this act of rubbing up the ball, they are then shown up as naughty boys. Derose added that Smith (rather like 'Little Hans', Freud's five-year-old patient) became 'Little Steve'; it was when he spoke of the pain his act had caused his 'old man' that Smith's sobbing became almost uncontrollable. At that moment, the hand of his father appeared on-screen on his shoulder, the hand of sympathy but also the hand of authority, disappointment and disapproval.

One might also see this entitlement in the players' naivety. There are twenty-four cameras at most big cricket matches. The jockstrap is an inadequate recourse if you're caught in the act! It was as if they felt they were so important – indeed omnipotent – that they would never be caught. 'We, the entitled, will get away with anything!' They may also have believed that the culture of the organisation (the only important thing is winning) might have excused them, that any culpability would be mitigated in the eyes of the cricketing authorities (and beyond). Australian cricketers had probably been exposed to sledging since their early teens. They had been brought up in a school that was not only hard but often ruthless.

The motto of winning at any cost needs to be resisted and modified. It is not the only proper aim. We rightly play to win but we don't play in order to win. In 2019, Ashley Giles, England's director of cricket, unveiled Chris Silverwood's appointment as head coach. Giles had asked a simple question of the prospective candidates on the shortlist: 'How does this England side become the most *respected* in the game?' Note: not 'the most successful'. (I'm reminded of times when I was asked to speak as captain of Middlesex at pre-season AGMs: my aim, I would say, was for the team to play *purposive* cricket: I did not promise either to 'entertain' or to 'win'.)

No-one expects that at top-level sport such behaviours and attitudes can be eradicated. We put twenty-two young men into a setting where rivalries and cultural differences have a long history, and we invite them to be full-hearted in their aggression. It is not easy to inhabit a cauldron of potential triumphalism and depression and be expected to behave as at a vicarage tea party (though I daresay vicarages are not exempt from similar attitudes, even without the sandpaper).

It is for reasons such as this that we need to remind ourselves of the spirit of cricket, not least in questioning an overall prevalent attitude.

CEO James Sutherland's announcement of the punishments handed down to Smith, Warner and Bancroft spoke of their 'acts against the spirit of the game, unbecoming of its representatives, harming its interests and bringing it into disrepute'; all true, but perhaps it would have helped to spell out more of the detail.

The scandal was a catalyst to at least one (small) change. Later that year, ICC 'promoted' 'changing the state of the ball' from a Level 2 to a Level 3 offence, along with other 'attempts to gain an unfair advantage'.

The punishment, of which the most painful part was the public disgrace, was not a mild one. And one feature of the longer game of cricket is that teams and individuals get a second chance. This principle needs to be applied to life in general. Cricket is played by human beings. We all have to learn to suffer and endure periods of impotence and vulnerability. Everyone is liable to backslide. And we all need, as I say, to be reminded of the spirit not only of cricket but of sport and of shared human endeavours. Sutherland spoke of the need to balance punishment with the chance of redemption. I agree. We all need justice to be both discriminating and tempered with mercy. And once the sentence has been served, once the debt to the cricketing world and to society at large has been paid, those concerned should be given a fresh start.

Two years on, we don't know if the breakdown into anguish and shame will lead to a breakthrough and a deep-seated change of heart, either in the individuals concerned, or in cricket in general. Sometimes galling experiences of this kind do make for a transformation in attitudes.

I was impressed with former England captain Nasser Hussain speaking on television after the First Test between England and Australia at Edgbaston in 2019 – a match in which Smith batted wonderfully well, scoring 142 and 144 to lead Australia to victory. Nasser said that he could not understand the mentality of those who would not forgive these young men for a mistake made, for which they had been punished severely and from which they had returned with dignity. We don't expect perfection of technique even from the greatest players. Should we expect perfect behaviour?

In fact, the whole Australian team behaved well in the series, not once complaining at bad luck. If they said anything on the field, they said it with a smile on their faces (Pat Cummins was aptly labelled 'The Grinning Assassin'). They got on the with the game. Which was more than could be said for some England supporters.

Vinoo Mankad, looking resigned . . .

2

WHY WOULD YOU EVEN THINK OF DOING SUCH THINGS?

'The urban and exacting idea of cricket as a bold theatre of aggression.'

Michael Billington on Harold Pinter's view of cricket

On Saturday 27 June 1964, Cambridge University began a three-day match against Kent at Folkestone. The weather was perfect. Kent showed us respect in picking a strong team – openers Peter Richardson and Mike Denness, Colin Cowdrey at four, Brian Luckhurst at seven, Alan Knott, and fast bowlers David Sayer and John Dye. (The latter got me out for the only 'pair' in my career, four weeks later, when I played for Middlesex against Kent at Lord's. Between the first dismissal on Saturday morning and the second on Monday evening the team for the MCC tour of South Africa had been announced, and I was in it.) I see that I was keeping wicket in the Folkestone match (which I'd forgotten but remembered clearly when seeing it on the online scorecard), as well as opening the batting.

Winning the toss, we batted. I scored a fluent 44, before playing an ungainly shot to an apparently harmless ball from a slow bowler to be caught at square leg. Jack Fingleton, the opener who played many Tests with Don Bradman, and who fell out with him, wrote in the *Sunday Times* that I had thrown away a great start . . . Cambridge scored 255; Kent replied with 244 for 8 declared. We then declared on 256 for 5 (Brearley 67) before setting Kent a target of 268 in what turned out to be 55 overs. In a tight finish, Kent won by 3 wickets.

I remember two moments from this last innings of the match. The first occurred when Cowdrey was batting. As our bowler started his run-up, I noticed that square leg was standing in the wrong place and moved him a couple of yards towards mid-wicket. Cowdrey realised something was going on and stepped away. It's against the ethics of the game to move fielders after the bowler has started his approach. I'm as sure as I can be that I wasn't trying to pull a fast one; rather I was more simply, but too casually, making a late adjustment to something I'd just noticed was not right. Undoubtedly, I should either have left the field as it was, or stopped the bowler in his run-up and moved the man at square leg in full view of the batsmen. What I did was wrong, not in a major way, but still wrong.

The second incident occurred at the very end of the match. Kent needed something like 12 runs in the last five minutes. In those days, there were no regulations insisting on a requisite number of overs that had to be bowled from the beginning of the last 'hour'; it was simply a matter of time running out. All four results were possible, though we had only an outside chance of winning. Richard Hutton, our medium-fast bowler, was bowling this over. I felt strongly that two overs should be bowled. After three balls, Hutton lost his run-up. He may even have stopped to tie up his bootlaces. It looked as though time would run out. To ensure the final over, I ordered him to bowl his last ball off a short run, He, perhaps feeling disgruntled, or aware of sore feet, lost his rhythm and bowled a full toss, which Knott hit for four. Kent won with three balls to spare.

So, within a small time frame, I had acted against the spirit of the game (moving a fielder after the bowler started his run-up); and according to its spirit (instructing the bowler to bowl off a short run). One was a matter of doing something behind a batsman's back; the other was maintaining a respect for time and for giving our opponents their due, even if it might result in our own defeat.

'Play hard but fair,' the spirit of the game recommends; or, as the frieze on the wall at the corner of Lord's has it (quoting the poet Henry Newbolt): 'Play up, play up, and play the game.'

Yes, indeed. But is there not too, alongside this impulse, a pull to ignore standards, towards easier, sometimes more deceptive, ruses, towards deceiving ourselves and others? Indeed, it may be the presence of this other tendency that elicits the need for high-minded prescriptions.

Decades later, I gave a talk to a group of students and colleagues at a venue in South London near the Maudsley Hospital. The topic was: 'Cricket and psychoanalysis: what is the point of sport?' I spoke of overlaps between the two fields, some of them not at first sight obvious. I touched on the need for both competition and cooperation. In the discussion I made a distinction between corruption and cheating. I don't think I mentioned the 'spirit of cricket', but this idea was in the background of my talk.

Afterwards, over a glass of wine, one of the analysts (I'll call her Christina) asked me to enlarge on this contrast. I had already suggested that corruption, as in match-fixing, or spot-fixing – that is, fixing a small part of a game – is much worse than what I call 'common-or-garden' cheating. The latter is a matter of trying to get an advantage within the game by either breaking or bending the rules, as in tax evasion or elaborate tax avoidance; it may involve breaking rules, or behaving in ways that appear to be consistent with the rules but are contrary to the intention behind them. Now I added that, in my view, everyone is tempted to break or bend rules, and many succumb to the temptation in small or large ways. Christina challenged me. 'Why would you want to do that?' she asked. 'Why would you or anyone even *think* of doing such things?'

This remark took me aback. I had assumed that we all have layers of weakness. We are all potential cowards, amenable to the lure of easy advantage. As a friend said: 'When it comes to temptation, we all have our limits, our thresholds for going against our principles, especially where disappointment, pain and humiliation are at stake, and when excitement or power, frequently related to sex or money, are to be grasped at.' And we all are inclined to take shortcuts, as I did when shifting (shiftily) square leg all those years go.

We are prone to deceiving, too, others and ourselves. I take it that learning to dissimulate is part of a two-year-old's growing up to be more independent. He or she discovers the importance of a private space: 'Me do it myself,' (s)he protests.

They tell lies – little lies, fibs – testing out ways of protecting themselves against failure, seeing how far they can go. Children, as they grow up, may lie because they are ashamed of themselves; or of their parents, wanting to protect them. Or, too confused to understand, they create a story that might more or less fit or compensate for the facts: 'Did you eat the cake, Johnny?' asks Mother, coming back into the kitchen. 'No,' says he, his face covered with sticky brown chocolate.

They may be secretly planning future deceptions: once, when I was ten or eleven, I was late home from school because the bus didn't come. I remember thinking: 'I can use that for an excuse one day if I've got late from playing football in the playground till dark.'

Many games involve winning and losing; children want to win, often desperately, and will if it suits them break the rules or invent new ones. Learning Scrabble, bilingual children use words from either language, or mongrel words, and place them where the score is tripled. Their capacity to dissemble is also in part an imitation of their elders; we adults tend to be economical with the truth, or to 'cheat'.

As children and as adults, our wishful thinking leads us to twist or turn reality, distorting how things are, often in ways that are hidden from ourselves. Parts of ourselves are foreign to us. As batsmen, we turn what had in fact been a foreseeable mode of dismissal into bad luck; we convert an ordinary delivery that we simply missed into an unplayable one. In a dream a patient turns his analyst into a robotic oil rig, relentlessly nodding its disapproval as it spies on his private space through his bedroom window. We are not exactly telling lies, except to ourselves.

Not all making things up is a matter of denial or deception. Even in being defensive or self-deceptive, we are creative in our ways of misconstruing self and other. Children *need* their own secrets, their privacy. They also use their imaginations. They want their own places, where only they can go, the magic wardrobe, the space apart, the secret garden. Tendencies to deceive are contiguous with shrewdness, innovativeness and creativity. All involve going beyond the accepted, or even the conventionally acceptable. The small child plays 'pretend', and learns to recognise and enjoy pretend-games. Watching the ballet *Peter and the Wolf*, our three-year-old granddaughter, anxious at the arrival of the wolf and seeking reassurance, whispered: 'They are *people*, aren't they? They *are* just pretending?' Illusion is an important ability as well as a danger or drawback. It was because of its attractiveness and the power of its appeal to the emotions that Plato banned poetry from his ideal state. Constructions of self and the world often involve complex and clever 'stories' ('telling a story' is, or was, a euphemism for lying).

But now, listening to Christina, I had to consider whether this attitude of mine was cynical, whether I was generalising from my own degenerate case.

My trickiness had come up in my analysis, naturally, but here it was put in a new form. Were others immune to such tendencies? Was I wrong to think of Christina's orientation as, inevitably, 'too good to be true'? Was it instead simply good? Is goodness itself simple?

Or are we fated, whether we understand ourselves or not, to be complex? And if so, was it that my interlocutor, Christina, was naive? Did she underestimate her own capacity for self-deception, which of course leads others to be deceived? It didn't feel like that, not at all. But I do ask: what had happened to her liability to reorganise the world to suit herself, both inside her head and in the complicated living of a life with all its frustrations and prohibitions?

I don't know the answer to these questions. But examining the topic of the 'spirit of cricket' is one route into wider questions about honesty, transparency and generosity; about deviousness, trickiness and cheating.

Thinking about this was what took me back to that match at Folkestone in 1964.

Most cricket people believe in, and advocate (sometimes with passion), playing within the spirit of the game. Even if in their words they deny the value or validity of this phrase, their actions and opinions reveal a belief in it (or in something like it). But what do we mean by the term?

'Spirit of cricket' has both an informal and a more formal sense. Formally, it is the title and substance of the Preamble to the Laws of Cricket. Informally, it originated as an expression of a public-school ethos. From the mid-nineteenth century, cricket became an epitome of nobility, of a muscular Christianity in which *mens sana* exists *in corpore sano* – a healthy mind needs a healthy body. There were class elements in this, with the emphasis on respect, often for rank, including the rank of captaincy, and for courtesy.

Not that this was entirely new. In the 1790s, Bray, a 'great centre of cricket', near Maidenhead, beat the aristocratic MCC XI, and 'had the church bells rung to celebrate their victory. This so enraged the visiting gentlemen that they refused to stay for the elaborate dinner that was to have followed the game.' Local patriotism was all very well, but had to be appropriately expressed.

'It's not cricket' became a byword for ungentlemanly behaviour. If someone tried to use 'it's not football', or even 'it's not golf', in a similar way, he or she would not be understood.

Alongside class, there was the issue of empire. Sport, often particularly cricket, prepared the gentry for ruling. Barbadian historian Keith Sandiford begins his piece on 'Cricket and Victorian Society' as follows:

> Cricket was much more than a game for the Victorians. They glorified it . . . as a perfect system of ethics and morals which embodied all that was most noble in the Anglo-Saxon character. They prized it as a national symbol, perhaps because . . . it was an exclusively English creation unsullied by Oriental or European influences. In an extremely xenophobic age, the Victorians came to regard cricket as further proof of their cultural supremacy.

Not that all Victorian cricketing heroes were paradigms of straightforwardness and honesty. The great W. G. Grace, in C. L. R. James's words 'the most famous Victorian of them all', was noted for his cunning, shrewdness and gamesmanship.

Two stories come to mind. One is the remark attributed to him when given out lbw: 'They haven't,' he is said to have told the umpire, 'come to see you umpire. They have come to see me bat.' The second was of a three-ball sequence from Essex fast bowler, Charles Kortright, at Leyton in 1898. Appeals for lbw and caught behind were turned down off the first two. Next ball, Kortright clean-bowled him. W. G. stood for a moment unbelieving, at which point the bowler said 'Surely you're not going, doctor? There's one stump still standing.' Grace felt insulted and refused to speak to him. W. G.'s pre-eminence implies a contrary trend in Victorian society, opposed to the public-school high-mindedness. And he was adored. We all (I think) admire, sneakily or otherwise, someone with the nerve to get away with it.

For some, even today, a love of cricket generates the idea that this game stands apart from the ambiguities of life, that it is less tainted by vice or hypocrisy. Somehow it is felt to be pure – the new pitch, the pleasant smell of freshly cut grass, the long-lived summer's day, the idyllic, nostalgic dream of rural bliss and timelessness. Adrian Stokes, who wrote eruditely about art and psychoanalysis, also wrote about cricket's countryside roots and its unconscious allusions, the white clothes gliding against a green background like cows in meadows, the gentle knock of the ball on the bat, the slow rhythms. But there are risks in the fantasies of purity and peacefulness, with its cosy images of village greens or grounds surrounded by trees and, as at Tunbridge Wells, rhododendrons.

Cricket is also nuggety, rugged, hard, passionate and urban. Harold Pinter called it a 'wonderfully civilized act of warfare', and 'a very violent game'.

My father Horace was the youngest of eight children in a working-class family living in Church Road, Heckmondwike, in the West Riding of Yorkshire. When he was ten, he made a pinhole camera, presumably at school. A rare surviving photo is of three cricket stumps painted on the industrially blackened wall that formed the back of their 'yard', and was part of the 'ginnel' (dialect for path or alley) between the rows of houses. From the age of seven or so, I had my own West London suburban version of these stumps. I would throw a tennis ball against the kitchen wall (aiming at, and usually hitting, the part just underneath the window), landing it on my carefully cut-and-rolled pitch, with three-dimensional stumps behind me, so that I could become Jack Robertson and other Middlesex heroes, awarding myself runs for shots played all round the wicket. My father's little photo carried a lot of meaning for me, as for him. It expressed the romance of his childhood in my mind and linked me with him and it. But there was another layer of emotion. For years I pressed him to help me make a pinhole camera. He did not demur. But somehow it was always the wrong time. The non-existence of the camera was my version of Virginia Woolf's *To the Lighthouse*, in which the promised trip to the alluring island, visible from the Skye holiday house the Ramsay family rented every summer, never happened. We never made a pinhole camera. And I can't find the picture now.

Horace (as we children called our father) was brought up in a tough school, cricket-wise as in other ways. I'm not certain that he would have 'walked' or advocated walking (voluntarily giving yourself out when you know you have edged the ball). I can't remember specific instances, nor can I remember him stating his views, whatever they were. This practice was de rigueur further south and in more genteel circumstances.

David Bloomfield, a team-mate of my father's in London in the 1950s, doesn't remember Horace waiting for such a decision. He says 'walking' was always a vexed issue, but matters have deteriorated since then, perhaps even because they now have independent umpires. Earlier there was more concern about mistakes being made by their own umpire! Implying that my father was one of them, he speaks of strong characters setting standards and playing the game 'properly'.

Certainly after the war, walking was standard practice in Yorkshire, not only among professionals but also in the leagues. Cricket writer Stephen Chalke got this clear impression from his long conversations with the great Yorkshire and England bowler, Bob Appleyard, who first played for the county in 1950. Chalke suggests that the northern way of life was less individualistic, upholding strong common values. And Bob Platt, the ex-Yorkshire opening bowler, who played ninety-six matches for the county between 1955 and 1963, and later became club president, also referred mainly to the mentality prevalent post-war when he said: 'We thought of not-walking as cheating. In the leagues too, we knew the cheats, and they were ostracised. This attitude permeated into the lower leagues.'

There was a caveat; according to Charlie Elliott, the ex-Derbyshire player whom I knew when he was an umpire and an England selector, walking had to be done promptly or not at all. If players were swiftly given not out, walking might have been seen as implicit criticism of the umpires, so they would then have stayed put. Jack Hobbs – a paragon of integrity – shared this view, Elliott added. When I mentioned the different attitude of Australian cricketers to walking, Platt told me that the Yorkshire players' reaction was: 'Aussies! They never walked but they accepted the umpire's decision. You can't argue with that.'

I remember from early days watching Horace play, and hearing his often-trenchant views, that he had clear ideas of right and wrong on the field. He strongly disapproved of bowlers deliberately bowling wide of the off stump, and would show his disgust. His disapproval had a moral or ethical dimension. According to him, such bowling was not an opportunity to smash the ball through the covers, it was purely negative. It was 'not done', it was 'bad form'. He would not have used the term 'against the spirit of cricket', but that is what he felt and believed with passion.

At a more sensitive level, he once quietly reprimanded me when I was captain of the school team for praising one of the players; this boy was a year senior to me, and I was slightly in awe of him. I was trying to please him. My father pointed out that my exaggerated praise might make it harder to take a clear-headed decision to drop him if that became appropriate later on.

He would also insist on his rights. I recently met someone who used to play against him in club cricket. He claimed to have enjoyed the fact that Horace was so stubborn and clear in what he thought was fair or right. If, when he was batting, bowlers alternated between bowling over and around the wicket, he would insist on having the sightscreen moved each time they changed, although this meant the fielders had to run to the screen and move it themselves.

I recall another incident, when Brentham played against the Indian Gymkhana on their ground in Osterley, Middlesex. There had been rain. One of the visiting batsmen, having played a defensive shot, went out to pat the pitch down. He was promptly run out. I imagine the umpire, following the letter of the law, gave him out on appeal. My father and the whole visiting team were outraged at this. They may even have dropped the fixture. Some at least of the home side must have considered it a fair dismissal; the batsman should wait until the ball is (thoroughly) 'dead' before leaving his crease.

I witnessed a similar event in a Test match at Johannesburg in 1965. Mike (M. J. K.) Smith, England captain, was the batsman, on 7. The South African wicketkeeper John Waite took a ball from Joe Partridge down the leg side, and in a single move passed it on to Pieter van der Merwe at backward short leg, who instantly threw down the stumps. Assuming the ball was dead, Smith had gone for a little wander, intending to flick away small bits of dirt from the pitch.

The current (2019) Law 20.1.1.1 states: 'The ball is dead when: it is finally settled in the hands of the wicket keeper or bowler', and 20.1.2: 'The ball shall be considered to be dead when it is clear to the bowler's end umpire that the fielding side and both batsmen at the wicket have ceased to regard it as in play.'

Smith was given out by umpire Hayward Kidson. South Africa's captain Trevor Goddard consulted with Waite and van der Merwe, talked to Kidson, who then recalled Smith (who went on to score 42).

My father's moral attitudes were not confined to sport. I remember him talking angrily about a stunt by Winston Churchill, presumably during the war. In order to persuade people to work harder and boost production, Churchill spent an hour bricklaying, then argued that his rate for an hour should be achieved pro rata over fifty or sixty hours' work a week. My father felt this was unfair, taking no account of the impact of fatigue. I'm confident he was right.

Platt said that in his playing days in Yorkshire: 'Cricket was a way of life, near to godliness via the Church of England.' Then he realised his companion, Father Felix of Ampleforth, was giving him a funny look.

And yet is cricket uniquely character-building? Does it more than other activities help us to be better persons? If so, should government policy make it a moral imperative to teach young people sport (even specifically cricket), as a way of preparing them for life, that it should be timetabled in all schools, perhaps ahead of music or drama or religion?

In all walks of life there are good and bad behaviours and attitudes. Everyone has to deal with rivalry and envy, with passive aggression and lethargy, with destructiveness of various kinds, in others if not ourselves. And in virtually all contexts there are standards of politeness and fair play, respect and acknowledgement of differing opinions, all of which make for good relationships and good teams. Even in the conduct of war, there are rules, accepted at least in principle, governing what is permissible.

Cricketers are not always paragons, nor should we expect them to be. Nor are other activities somehow less humanising.

Let me, though, offer some possible arguments for what cricket can offer.

The first is that cricket (along with baseball) is unique among team games in that each little episode of the drama – each delivery from bowler to batsman – is primarily a one-to-one contest situated within a team context. In no other team game are individual scores and performances so capable of being statistically recorded, on scoreboards and in scorecards, for the perusal of the public. Goal-scorers in soccer, try-scorers in rugby, get their mentions and headlines, but no one supposes that the only significant contribution to their teams' success is their finishing off what led to these moments of personal glory, whereas in cricket there may be sound reason for such inferences. Perhaps, then, cricketers have a more complicated task within the team than most other sportsmen, having to learn to mature to a stage where they can on the whole enjoy their team-mates' successes and sympathise with their failings, without losing necessary individual, even selfish, ambitions.

34

Second, when dismissed for a low score, the cricket batsman suffers a starker sense of loss than in other games and other pastimes. Whereas a musician giving a concert doesn't have to stop after playing a wrong note, the batsman, thanks to a single mistake or a single delivery, is permanently cut off, a king deposed, often before his reign has got going. Sometimes surviving at the crease is more painful than a quick dismissal. There are slow tortures as well as slow deaths, and it takes grit and deep confidence to survive being made to look inept in public. If one can learn to bear the pain of a run of low scores without denying that it matters but also without long-term despair, without too many delusions, this may be character-building.

Third, there are the traditions themselves, and the fact that despite the snobbery, despite Sandiford's sharp and accurate point that cricket was seen as 'proof of cultural supremacy', it also provided, gradually, against a current of ongoing prejudice, in the West Indies as elsewhere, a relatively level playing field. 'They are no better than we,' C. L. R. James wrote in 1933, quoting Learie Constantine.

Entering into the form of life that is cricket one enters into such values alongside the requirement of skills. I don't of course mean that we immediately embrace these values, nor that all these traditions are admirable or self-evident; but we will imbibe and come to believe in them; and some of the traditions are indeed admirable.

Positive attitudes, some of them referred to in the Preamble to the Laws – enjoying our team-mates' successes, being good losers, respecting umpires, captains and the opposition, and so on – do indeed tend to influence and even inform our approach, not only in the cricket context but beyond.

But we are also prone to very different group and individual feelings – of envy, resentment, humiliation, triumph, which may override the more cooperative ones. Sport is graceful *and* raw (as Pinter said). Both mindsets are, I think, inevitable – and, within limits, valuable. My own experience and observation persuade me that the solidarity of team spirit and hard-but-fair competitive play is stronger than that of boorishness inspired by tribal rivalry. And such solidarity need not infringe too much on each individual's freedom and creativity. I'm inclined to think that the good outweighs the bad, but it's not a one-horse race!

One more question: if sport influences our attitudes to life beyond the game, and if, as seems obviously true, life in general influences how we are in the smaller parts of life, like playing sport, am I offering an account of the former or the latter?

My answer is: both. Certainly the broader self, the whole self, is bound to influence the part-self, the self that plays roles within different fields of life or institutions. As D. H. Lawrence said: 'The soul of man is a dark vast forest, with wild life in it.' Clearly, too, the part may influence the whole, for better or for worse. So I'm relaxed about their mutuality.

For most, cricket, like music or dancing, is a leisure activity. It is part of life, though set apart from the pragmatics of life. Carrying over the lessons of our recreations may be real and reliable. But these domains are simpler and more boundaried than the rough and tumble of family life. Values learned there, however real and important, may be left at the bar or the field. Perhaps being a good team-mate is hard to maintain. Emotions are more difficult to control at home. Some men come home and kick the cat, or harass the wife and children. Bonhomie, benevolence and respect are replaced by silence, surliness and uninterest.

But not always! Maybe Camus integrated what he had learned on the football field, evolving from there into a better human being in the living of his life.

3

IF WE WANT THINGS
TO STAY AS THEY ARE

'Crafty persons [have] invented new . . . games by reason
whereof archery is sore decayed.'

Unlawful Games Act 1541

'Everyone plays it [the game they call "cricket"], the
common people and also men of rank.'

Cesar de Saussure, French traveller in England, 1727

Cricket has long been thought of as the epitome of fair play. It is
striking how many cricketing phrases have entered into our everyday
language. Its terms became embedded in language that housed its
values. 'Not cricket' portrays behaviour or attitudes that are felt to be
disreputable; whereas 'keeping a straight bat' means playing according
to basic rules, maintaining your cool and your politeness, keeping to
your main points and your own style despite provocation (though it
can veer into something more negative, like 'stonewalling', a country
metaphor applied to batting, and then to obstructive defensiveness).
'My son had an idea for a film, went ahead and made it "off his own
bat"', that is, he did it without much assistance from anyone else.
A government minister might 'take his eye off the ball', 'be put on the
back foot' or 'stumped for an answer' – left high and dry by a wily verbal

challenge, like a batsman stranded, out of his ground, by a *'googly'* from a canny spin bowler, who conceals his main point by giving an impression of predictability or innocence. Even the word *'spin'* hints at cricketing derivation. Similarly, *'playing on a sticky wicket'* means having to deal with tricky situations in life. A health worker recently referred to a patient as having been *'hit for six'* by Covid-19.

What falls under spirit is harder to pin down than what is prescribed or proscribed by law. In cricket and beyond, there are overlaps and differences between spirit and law. Justice, for instance, is a concept wider and harder to define than law. Virtue and grace in life raise deeper questions than doing one's duty. We need clear rules, but we also need to question them. Spirit is broader than simply obeying the letter of the law.

Law and spirit are different from each other, and yet they overlap. Even the rule of law calls for consideration of the purposes of the law, and of how the proper intentions of the lawmakers apply in individual cases.

Some disputes, in cricket and outside it, are best solved by introducing legally binding laws or regulations, and thus more definitive grounds for decision. For instance, wides had to be penalised to stop the negative practice of bowling too wide for the batsman to reach the ball. And there was one batsman who manufactured a bat broader than the stumps. Such stalemates had to be outlawed. And even in these and similar cases the criteria for changes of law were broadly moral, for the betterment of the game, to avoid deadlock or danger. Sometimes law changes ratified changes that had already largely crept into practice, as with the advent of round-arm bowling.

The millennial edition of the Laws of Cricket, published by MCC, custodians of the Laws since the late eighteenth century, appeared with a new Preamble in which the spirit of cricket was given official status prefatory to the detailed rules (laws) of the game. The current edition of this Preamble, from 2017, reads as follows:

> *Cricket owes much of its appeal and enjoyment to the fact that it should be played not only according to the Laws, but also within the Spirit of Cricket.*
>
> *The major responsibility for ensuring fair play rests with the captains, but extends to all players, match officials and, especially in junior cricket, teachers, coaches and parents.*
>
> *Respect is central to the Spirit of Cricket.*
>
> *Respect your captain, team-mates, opponents and the authority of the umpires.*
>
> *Play hard and play fair.*
>
> *Accept the umpire's decision.*
>
> *Create a positive atmosphere by your own conduct, and encourage others to do likewise.*
>
> *Show self-discipline, even when things go against you.*
>
> *Congratulate the opposition on their successes, and enjoy those of your own team.*
>
> *Thank the officials and your opposition at the end of the match, whatever the result.*
>
> *Cricket is an exciting game that encourages leadership, friendship and teamwork, which brings together people from different nationalities, cultures and religions, especially when played within the Spirit of Cricket.*

How did cricket get to this point? What is law for, and how does the Preamble fit in? What are we to make of this rather odd introduction, preliminary to the Laws, which briefly gives space for competitiveness and passion ('play hard') while at the same time advocating playing 'fair', that is, within the Laws and within the idea of justice or fairness, but then proceeds to address issues that have nothing to do with the Laws or fair play – urging us to thank the umpires and opposition for the game, and enjoy the successes of our team-mates?

* * *

Undifferentiated but varied forerunners of at least seven games – cricket, croquet, golf, bowls and skittles, rounders, baseball (or softball) and hockey (on ice or land) – presumably played mostly by boys, existed in unorganised ways for many centuries. Much of the early evidence refers to activities in south-east England; there is also a reference (in 1478) to a game of *'criquet'* near Saint-Omer in northern France. The essential features were: an implement (bat or stick – *'cricce'* was the Anglo-Saxon for crooked stick or staff, used by shepherds), a ball and a target (a wicket, goal or hole). Rules, often relatively local, would have gradually seeped in to settle disputes or preclude too much danger. In 1624, one Jasper Vinall was killed in Sussex, when a batsman attempted to hit the ball twice to avoid being caught; this may have been the occasion when obstructing the field first became outlawed.

Games going under the name of cricket were by the sixteenth century sufficiently prevalent for the playing of them to have been banned by an Act of Parliament instituted during the reign of Henry VIII, because 'crafty persons [have] invented new . . . games by reason whereof archery is sore decayed'. Cricket historian Rowland Bowen questions this, suggesting that the inference that this comment applied to cricket is unwarranted. Nevertheless, similarly motivated bans on football had been instituted in 1349 and 1477, focusing on the need for 'every strong and able-bodied person to practise with the bow' for reasons of national defence. What is certain is that the playing of cricket on the Sabbath was punishable by law. In 1640, cricketers were found guilty of this offence in a court at Maidstone, Kent. Legal records from 1598 contain a deposition by one John Derrick, then aged fifty-nine, that as a boy 'with diverse of his fellows, he did runne and play at crickette . . . on a parcell of land . . . near the Free Schoole at Guildford'.

The laws banning games were more likely to be breached than observed, and when they were used, the primary purpose seems to have been to restrict riotous or unsavoury gatherings. In 1629, a curate from Ruckinge, on the edge of Romney Marsh in Kent, having been criticised for playing cricket, felt he needed to defend its respectability, saying that 'it was a game played by persons of repute and fashion'. But it was not until more than two hundred years later, in 1845, that 'an amending Act relieved games of skill of their shackles [of illegality] and only then did MCC and cricket become honest members of society', as R. S. Rait Kerr put it in his history of the laws of cricket.

During the Commonwealth of 1649–60, aristocrats retreated to their country seats, where village cricket became a locus for playing for stakes (though they were often small). After the Restoration, they, together with members of the nobility, brought cricket back to London, in particular to the Artillery Ground in Finsbury Fields. Large, sometimes huge, stakes were now placed on games, in some cases amounting to 1,000 guineas, rising exceptionally to 4,000 guineas (approximately £1 million today) by the end of the eighteenth century.

Gambling was not always above board. Cricket at Hambledon, a small village in Hampshire, began around 1744. Between 1772 and 1796, Hambledon won thirty-six of their seventy-one matches against All England, Kent, Surrey and Sussex. 'Hambledon' became the name for an era of cricket. John Nyren, whose memories of the cricketers of his father's time as a prominent Hambledon player were published in 1833, admitted that crooked practices were to be found among the younger players. By 1820, the selling of matches was rife. Shortly afterwards, MCC banned bookmakers from Lord's cricket ground.

The prospect of money, to be gained or lost, had long focused minds on playing conditions or rules.

On 11 July 1727, earlier than any evidence we have of a code of laws, 'Articles of Agreement', were drawn up between the Duke of Richmond and his opponent, one Mr Brodrick, to cover two prospective matches to be played between their teams that summer, one in Surrey and the other in Sussex.

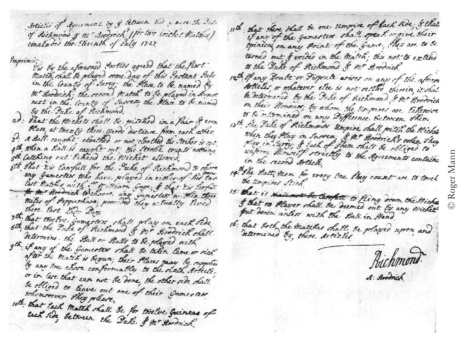

© Roger Mann

This document not only laid down arrangements for the matches – the choice of venues and pitches, the qualifications for players on each side, the appointment and roles of umpires, the stakes involved – it also stated rules for the playing of the game itself, including for certain dismissals. The length of the pitch was to be twenty-three yards – surprisingly, since the agricultural chain (twenty-two yards) had long been in use for this purpose. What was to constitute a 'run' was defined: a run was completed 'when the batsman touched the umpire's stick or bat with his bat'; and run-outs required the ball to be in the hand of the person breaking the wicket. Several articles specify what was to count as a fair catch. For example, when the ball was caught, no runs were to be scored for the stroke leading to dismissal; further, a batsman was to be out if a ball was caught 'cloathed or not cloathed'; and finally, catches behind the wicket were allowed. (The meaning of 'cloathed' is not clear. It might refer to dismissals being allowed if the ball is hugged to the fielder's clothes, or it might refer to the ball being 'clothed' in leather.)

The agreement dealt too with requirements on conduct. Any 'gamesters' (i.e. players) who 'shall speak or give an opinion' (I presume about an umpire's decision) 'are to be turned out and voided in the match'. It added that this provision did not apply to the Duke or to Mr Brodrick – in other words the captains (or 'owners'?) were to be allowed to question or challenge an umpire, but no one else was.

It seems likely that these Articles referred to playing conditions that differed from what were by then generally accepted rules (or laws) of the game. It is possible that there was already a master code, maintained at the Artillery Ground, not substantially changed but simply revised in the code adopted in 1744. The articles in the 1727 agreement would, on this assumption, have been included in order to clarify in advance potential points of contention about laws that had previously existed, but were disputed, unclear or locally varied.

More generally, it is possible that around 1750 the responsibility (and right) to alter the Laws may have devolved from the small group of those playing at the Artillery Fields earlier in the century to the Hambledon club. In 1771, for instance, a committee of Hambledon players took matters into their own hands, deciding to limit the width of the bat – though it is not clear whether this requirement applied other than locally. What is known is that whatever prestige with regard to laws that the club may have had was handed to the MCC soon after the latter's inception in 1787. Many of the leading members at Hambledon were also founding members of MCC.

From 1787 to the present, this one body (MCC) has been the single and continuous authority vis-à-vis the Laws. There has grown over time a deeper sense of constitutionalism, with recognition of the need for worldwide consultation on proposed changes, recognising cricket's expansion and the resultant variety in climatic and cultural conditions; and for promulgation of proposed law-changes months before a decision is to be taken (to give room for second thoughts, for instance about unintended consequences). Consultation has also expanded to include a wider range of interested and knowledgeable parties, including umpires, administrators and players.

For all forms of cricket, and in cricket at every level, the requirements for dismissals, for umpires and signals, for scorers, for pitch, creases and so on, for run-scoring and boundaries, for no balls and most extras – apply universally.

The Laws are, however, not definitive across the whole game. Every competition has 'playing regulations' that are layered on top of the Laws. Those involving international cricket are written not by MCC but by ICC, those concerning first-class cricket in the UK by the England and Wales Cricket Board (ECB). Russell Cake (recently chair of MCC's Laws subcommittee) suggests that cricket is the only sport that has at international level this mixture of rules and playing conditions, written by different bodies.

And there is an awkward anomaly: the Laws – the bedrock or the game – do not specifically address or even acknowledge the existence of limited-overs cricket, though it is probable that the majority of cricket matches played today are in this category. The lawmakers felt that to do so would make the combination of Laws and playing regulations too complicated. 'Time' cricket has the fewest restrictions,

Cake told me, 'so the simpler solution was to have the Laws as the bedrock, with all limited-overs conditions written into playing regulations'. Thus the Laws do not include aspects central to this form of the game, such as the removal of logical place for one possible result, the draw. Nor do the Laws refer to the various restrictions that are applied in limited-overs cricket – in overall numbers of overs, in fielders allowed within certain areas, in numbers of overs allowed to be bowled by any individual, in the definition of wides, in questions about the permissibility of declarations. All these and other issues specific to limited-overs matches are dealt with in playing regulations under the authority of various administrative bodies.

This anomaly became in a way less prominent once limited-overs cricket among first-class cricketers (starting in the early 1960s) became more prevalent, since local conditions have tended to model themselves on the regulations operating at the higher level, and have thus become more standardised. Many countries take as the regulations for their local 50-over competitions ICC's playing regulations for international 50-over cricket; likewise with T20 regulations. In England, however closely they rely on regulations in the professional game, most leagues write their own playing conditions. The principle is: 'Laws of cricket apply *except* . . . ' Then each league, local or national, states its exceptions, which become more copious as you get to younger age groups.

It would be wise, I think, for lawmakers to refer to this anomaly in a preface to the Laws.

* * *

But what have been the broad categories of criteria for changes in the Laws of cricket? I would say there have been four main sorts of reason. One is to maintain or restore balance and fairness between bowler and batsman, some of the imbalances deriving from technological changes. The second is what we might call vitality as opposed to negativity, including attempts to defeat unduly defensive strategies and manoeuvres. The third criterion is safety. A fourth ground for change has been consistency and clarity. Often, the motto of novelist Giuseppe di Lampedusa in *The Leopard* applies: 'If we want things to stay as they are' (or as they previously were, before insidious obstacles entered in), 'things will have to change'.

Here are examples of each kind of criterion. First, the advent of the third stump (at some date between 1755 and 1785: it was in the Laws of 1785) prevented the anomaly arising from the two-stump wicket that the ball sometimes went straight through the wicket without hitting either stump and thus without dislodging the bail. This was clearly unfair to the bowler. 'Lumpy' Stevens, a famous Hambledon cricketer, complained that he was in this way unfairly deprived of wickets on several occasions in a single match at the Artillery Ground in 1755. Recognition of the injustice of this incongruity led to the gradual introduction, in all important games, of the third stump over the ensuing few years.

A further example occurred in 2019, when restrictions were introduced for the first time to the maximum permitted depth of the bat, and the maximum thickness of its edges. The aim was to help rebalance the game at a time when bat-making improvements, shorter boundaries and more aggressive batsmanship had resulted in more and more mishits going for six.

The second criterion applied in 1810 when for the first time the batting side was credited with an automatic run when a wide was delivered. Before the penalty was introduced, some bowlers had made a mockery of the game by bowling the ball so wide that the batsman could not reach it – a ruse that might win a bet, but was certainly unfair and against the spirit of the game. Something had to be done to prevent stalemates resulting from such utterly negative cricket.

An example of a Law change based on this criterion arose when the bat's width was restricted to 4¼ inches, a limit that is still in place. Nyren is quoted as saying: 'Several years since, I do not remember the exact date, a player named White of Ryegate, brought a bat to a match which, being the width of the stumps, effectually defended his wicket from the bowler.' The new Law precluded this purely defensive and negative resort.

The third factor – safety – was one of the issues at stake in the long controversies culminating in the legalising of, first, round-arm bowling (in 1828) and, second, over-arm bowling (in 1864). One of the arguments advocating that the game stay with under-arm bowling was that round-arm bowling was too 'rough', that is, too dangerous. Today the umpire is instructed to warn and, for a second offence in the same innings, suspend a bowler if he deems it likely that a batsman, taking account of his level of skill, will be injured by the bowler's short-pitched bowling (Law 41).

As for the fourth criterion, there have long been efforts to find a definition of 'throwing' that is both clear and accurate. And today there is a debate about whether 'Mankading' should continue to appear under the 'Fair and Unfair Play' section of the Laws, or whether it should be moved to the section governing run-outs.

As with the law of the land, the aim of justice or fairness lies behind many of the motives for change, though inevitably there are interests that may consciously or unconsciously affect the attitudes of lawmakers. The balance between batsmen and bowlers may, for example, tend to be tilted towards the former; ex-batsmen predominate among the lawmakers, as will generally have been the case, given that those lawnmakers usually came from the more privileged members of society, by whom batting has often been regarded as a more leisurely and therefore more gentlemanly activity than the sweaty labour involved in bowling. ('Shout down a pit and up would come a fast bowler,' used to be said in coal-mining towns in the north of England, just as later in the West Indies the saying went: 'Shake a palm tree and a fast bowler falls out'.) Similarly, in society at large the balance between rich and poor may be unfairly influenced by the fact that most judges and MPs are more affluent and from more privileged backgrounds than the average.

As in the law of the land, changes in the social environment (such as swifter methods of travel and of publicity) and in technology (for instance, improvements in pitch-making techniques including the replacement of sheep as grazers by lawnmowers, or more recently in bat-making and in the opportunities for ball-tracking) have interacted mutually with changes in law and playing regulations.

Throughout the first part of the nineteenth century there were passionate debates about what should be permissible in bowling actions. There were those who wanted to give the bowler more freedom, whether by allowing him to 'throw' (that is, to jerk his arm at the elbow in delivery, as in baseball) or to raise the hand at the point of delivery (first to round-arm, then to over-arm). These were contentious matters. Were umpires already turning a blind eye to the rules against them? Was there a need to give the bowler more? Did the advent of these forms of bowling make the game more interesting? Did they arise out of, and also necessitate, better-prepared pitches?

On the other hand, the advent of these faster and bouncier types of bowling did undoubtedly result in greater danger and 'rougher' or 'wilder' bowling. Was this desirable? In 1845, MCC gave the benefit of doubt on 'no-balls' to the batting side, and six years later instructed umpires to call no-ball if they so much as *suspected* a bowling action to be unfair. Nevertheless, in 1864 MCC granted 'complete emancipation to the bowlers', emancipation not from the prohibition against throwing, but from that against bowling over-arm.

The legalisation of these new forms of bowling was the result also of the spread of the game, and the great increase in the number of matches played; pitches were regularly becoming more reliable and on the whole safer for batting.

Innovations generally have unforeseen consequences, which themselves require other changes. In the earliest known version of the Laws (1744), there was no lbw rule. Presumably, the pronounced curve in the shape of bats meant that, like hockey players, batsmen stood back from the line of the ball in order to hit it. There were no pads or leg-guards at this time. Soon, however, the intentional use of the body to block the ball led to the first introduction of the lbw rule: in 1774 a batsman could be out lbw for 'putting his leg before the wicket with the design to stop the ball'. Fourteen years later the use of pads as a second line of defence led to a change in the Laws to enable the batsman to be out in this way even if he had no 'design' to kick it away, provided that the ball pitched and hit his leg (or other body-part) in line with the stumps; now there was no need for umpires to interpret intention. Over the years this remained the case, except that clarification was needed to define what was meant by 'delivered in a straight line to the wicket' – the ball had to pitch in the rectangle connecting leg stump at one end to off stump at the other. Later still, in 1937, as scores in first-class cricket increased, intention was re-introduced when the Law was changed to allow the batsman to be out lbw if the ball pitched outside off stump, provided that he either played no stroke, or that (if he played a stroke) the ball struck the pad in line with the stumps. This change led to less defensive use of the pads, though some batsmen against some bowlers made an art form of appearing to play a shot but in fact kicking the ball away – most notoriously during the stand of 411 by Peter May and Colin Cowdrey to counter the threat of the West Indian spinner Sonny Ramadhin, whom they couldn't read, in the 1957 series in England.

It will be seen that Law changes and controversies about lbw were about the avoidance of negativity and the restoration of balance between batsman and bowler.

* * *

There are many differences between the spirit and the letter of the law. In this chapter, however, I emphasise an important overlap: the point of the Laws of the game, and the purpose of typical Law changes, is centrally rooted in aspects of fairness, that is, in the spirit of the game. In general, Laws aim to provide the best possible arrangements for keeping or restoring a satisfying, interesting balance between bat and ball. Some Laws are brought in specifically to outlaw or restrict a strategy felt to be against the spirit.

In the 1958 edition of the *Wisden Cricketers' Almanack*, for instance, there is a first mention of the restriction on the number of fielders allowed behind square on the leg side. In a section after the Laws, an Experimental Note to Law 44 reads: 'The number of leg-side fielders shall not exceed five, of whom not more than two may be behind the popping crease at the instant of the bowler's delivery.' The recent focus on inswing bowling, aiming at leg stump, was offensive to many purists. The experiment also made the defensive strategy of bowling wide of leg stump less attractive. There is an intrinsic, physiological asymmetry in batting: while it is possible to play a wide range of proper cricket strokes to balls well outside the off stump (*pace* my father), the range of options is far more restricted in playing balls outside the leg stump.

The innovation may also have been belatedly designed to make the strategy of 'bodyline', the famous (or infamous) policy designed by Douglas Jardine to contain and restrict Don Bradman during England's tour of Australia in 1932–3, less attractive to bowlers and fielding captains, if not to rule it out altogether.

* * *

Games usually have 'rules', not 'laws' (though the 1775 edition of *Hoyle's Games Improved*, which dealt with games from cards to billiards, included 'The Laws of several Games as settled and agreed to at White's and Stapleton's Chocolate Houses'). For reasons that are not clear to me or, it seems, to others closely involved in working on them in recent years, cricket has continued to name its rules 'laws', which is how the first-known code, printed on a handkerchief in 1744, referred to them.

By contrast, during MCC's time as the guardian or custodian of the Rules of Tennis (the All England Club becoming involved only from 1880), what it produced in 1875 was a standardised set of *rules*. These were definitely 'rules' not 'laws'.

In general, rules are constitutive or definitive of a game. The rules of chess, for example, define what chess is. Beyond their definitional role, both laws and rules are instituted to avoid anarchy or chaos, to regularise the activities of life. Both enforce values and expectations. Both are concerned with safety and keeping a balance between opposing interest groups or tendencies. In everyday life, rules tend to be more informal, personal and locally variable than laws, which latter are often instituted by governments, and involve codes laying down sanctions and tariffs relating to the punishments to be imposed for breaking them. But this is also true, within a game, of rules.

I suspect that, in using the somewhat portentous term '*Laws* of Cricket', cricket wished to differentiate itself from other games, as if this English game was to stand above those regulated by potentially arbitrary 'rules' laid down by the powerful without debate or consensus. Perhaps already there was an appropriation of cricket's ethical superiority (via its gentlemanly manners) above other sports.

One reason for cricketers to feel this sense of entitlement may have been grounded in a reality – in the socially benign aspects of cricket. The game has been a social cement in England. It has long been played by every rank in villages and countryside, though for most of its history almost exclusively by men and boys. Novels like Charles Dickens's *The Pickwick Papers*, and Hugh de Sélincourt's *The Cricket Match*, as well as the autobiographical cricket matches described by Siegfried Sassoon in his *Memoirs of a Fox-Hunting Man*, all demonstrate this feature, often with a lacing of sentimentality. 'If everything about England was destroyed except for the laws of cricket,' wrote Neville Cardus, 'English society could be recreated.' In a more sardonic tone, George Orwell undercuts this rosy view with: 'Our abiding sense of an English village scene on a summer's day when, as the light fails, a ball hit for four kills a rabbit on the boundary.'

By the mid-nineteenth century the influx to cities produced by the Industrial Revolution brought cricket to every kind of location. The urban game was played by factory and other workers on their evenings off, or on Saturday afternoons. The game became tougher, less casual, more systematised. The railways meant that it was possible to travel fast between conurbations. Cricket grew in two main ways: among workers and artisans, and in the public schools and among the gentry, many of whom lived in and played in the country where the old rural game also continued.

Social historian G. M. Trevelyan wrote that if the French noblesse had been able to play cricket with their peasants the French Revolution would never have occurred. This is no doubt a dubious dictum, but nevertheless it's interesting that this argument could be presented in a serious book of social history. Cricket at its best offers a 'level playing field'.

So, despite colonial and class prejudices, cricket had some right to claim that its ethos, along with and partly embodied in its Laws, supported fair play, and represented a 'spirit' of mutual respect and acceptance. Much that is admirable is summed up in the public-school ethos, as represented by Rudyard Kipling in his famous poem 'If', and indeed most of these values would be subscribed to by cricketers, including rank-and-file professionals, of every social class.

*   *   *

The question remains: why the Preamble? And why was it introduced in 2000, a marker for the new millennium?

Ted Dexter and Colin Cowdrey, both ex-captains of England, both also ex-presidents of MCC had become alarmed at increasing numbers of reports, many from umpires, of abuse, sledging and unsporting behaviour, especially in club cricket, and even more shockingly, in schools. They noted that there was little or no reference to the spirit of the game in the Laws, and decided to put their ideas in the form of a Preamble, rather than within the Laws, as attempting to do the latter would require the palaver of a Special Meeting of the membership of MCC. They also initiated an annual 'Spirit of Cricket' lecture.

4

SHEEP

'They were that nice to us in New Zealand and we were that uncomfortable. I said in the team meeting: "I can't stand for this any more. We're going at them as hard as we can."'

Brad Haddin, Australian cricketer, 2015

'Mankading' (or 'Browning') is not a clear-cut issue, as we have seen. It is not always easy to sort the sheep from the goats. Appropriately enough, New Zealand, which once had twenty sheep to each human (now reduced to a mere seven to one), count as sheep for this purpose.

Playing in the right spirit is at times as infectious as is its opposite. New Zealand have over the past decade or so shown just such an admirable spirit, and this has influenced, in differing directions, their opponents and the wider game.

Neither side contesting the twelfth ICC World Cup Final in July 2019 had ever won this competition. New Zealand had been finalists only once, in 2015, when they lost by a wide margin to Australia in Melbourne; they had lost their other four semi-finals. England had lost all three finals – in 1979 at Lord's, in 1987 in Kolkata, and in 1992 in Melbourne.

New Zealand have regularly had one or two world-class players – Glenn Turner, Richard Hadlee, Martin Crowe, Shane Bond and Kane Williamson – along with several very good players. Usually they lack depth of talent. The (human) population numbers half that of London, perhaps a fifth of the number living in Mumbai. Graham Gooch once said that batting against New Zealand in Hadlee's day meant facing world-class bowling at one end, Ilford Third XI at the other. Unkind but incisive.

But they have often compensated for this lack of depth by sound common sense, by playing to their limitations, and by excellent fielding; overall, they have punched above their weight.

In 2019, New Zealand's semi-final victory over India – joint favourites with England – was a case in point. They batted laboriously, Ross Taylor scoring at less than a run every two balls, leaving a lot to the last few overs. It seemed that Williamson's dismissal resulted from his having had to take one risk too many to compensate. But Taylor came good the longer he batted, ending up with 74 off 90 balls, and in their 50 overs New Zealand reached a total (239 for 8) that gave them a chance on a pitch that had been played on before, on which the ball was taking spin and 'holding' – that is, not skidding through in a way that would have made smooth stroke-play, or even hitting, reliably safe. They then dismissed India's top three batsmen for one run each, and in the end, despite a wonderful late flurry by Jadeja (77 off 59 balls) in partnership with an M. S. Dhoni, whose 50 off 72 balls was sad to watch in the sense it gave of his being a shadow of the cool assassin he had once been, won by 18 runs.

Afterwards Taylor commented: 'We scrapped. That's what we always do.' This is true; but as well as scrapping, they had also made a shrewd calculation of what could well be a good enough score. At one stage in India's innings, their young slow left-arm bowler, Mitchell Santner, had taken 2 wickets for 7 runs in his first 6 overs.

For the final, England were rightly considered favourites. A dismal performance in the previous World Cup in 2015 had led to a new approach, initiated first by Andrew Strauss (England's director of cricket) and wholly embraced by captain Eoin Morgan and coach

Trevor Bayliss. Batting without fear, they became a team to be feared. Their openers – Jason Roy and Jonny Bairstow – sparked each other off; and the battering power of all-rounders Ben Stokes, Jos Buttler and Moeen Ali, along with Morgan himself, often held together by the excellent skill, sense and reliability of Joe Root, meant that on good pitches they almost always scored over 300. The bowling was impressive too. Crucially, recent changes in qualification rules meant that after three years of playing for Sussex, fast bowler Jofra Archer (born in Barbados) had qualified for England. With the new ball, he and Chris Woakes were both penetrative and hard to score off. They were followed by three who could take wickets in the middle overs and towards the end – Mark Wood, Liam Plunkett and Adil Rashid. And their fielding, as with most of the current teams, was top-class. England had had their hiccoughs during the competition, but entered the final with three fine victories against top sides in their last three games.

The balance of power in the final oscillated. New Zealand, surprisingly to me, decided to bat first on a cloudy morning with a tinge of green in the pitch. Once again, they scrapped. The ball passed the bat from time to time. One imagined that 241 was 20 or 30 runs below par. But England too struggled with the bat, their best batsman, Root, restricted to 7 off 30 balls. Colin de Grandhomme, who bowls at a modest military-medium pace, conceded only 25 runs in his 10 overs, bowled in a single spell that held England back. When Buttler joined Stokes (at 86 for 4), England needed 136 from almost 27 overs. While Buttler timed and placed the ball from the beginning, Stokes's placements were less sure. The run rate rose. New Zealand were fielding brilliantly (as indeed England had done earlier). The target reached 7 an over off the last 5 overs. At this point England looked (marginally) the favourites, but Buttler's dismissal swung the game the other way. With nine balls to go, Stokes hit the ball high to wide long on; Trent Boult held the catch, but trod on the boundary with his back foot before managing to throw the ball into the air as he fell backwards. His team-mate Martin Guptill caught it but instantly signalled six.

Despite this, fifteen were needed off the last over. With two balls left Stokes dived in for a second run; the ball struck his bat, and deflected to the boundary for four overthrows. As soon as it hit his bat, Stokes held up his arms to show that he had no intention of running for overthrows. The umpires signalled six (four for the overthrow, two for runs completed). This may have been a mistake. The Laws state that in such a case the runs to be counted (apart from the boundary) should depend on whether the batsmen have crossed at the moment the ball was released by the fielder. No cricketer or ex-cricketer I've spoken to knew this Law. England should have scored five; and Stokes would have been at the non-striker's end. The Law is unclear – suppose there is a relay of fielders throwing the ball in, which person's throw counts from the point of view of 'completed runs'? – more fundamentally, why should that be the factor? But whether or not the Law, or indeed the playing conditions for this competition (which determined the outcome in case of a tie), were the best imaginable, they had to be followed.

Aided by this colossal piece of luck, Stokes managed to squeeze 14 off the over. This led to the equivalent of the penalty shoot-out, the 'Super-over'. It too was tied, on 15 each. Once again, many knowledgeable observers were at a loss about the regulations for this improbable outcome – namely, that the winners were to be the side that had scored more runs *in boundaries* in the course of the game - England, as it turned out – as if five £20 notes were to be regarded as of more value than ten tenners!

Whatever we might think, in retrospect, about these matters, the spirit of cricket was shown at its best, both by Stokes's instinctive reaction to the overthrows and by Guptill's immediate response to Boult's having trodden on the boundary. Even more was it expressed by New Zealand's acceptance of defeat. Their disappointment was naturally palpable, but they displayed no truculence or outrage, despite the excruciating bad luck and the (possible) mistake by the umpires.

What happened in these last stages of the game – two ties, one after the 50 overs, the other in the 'Super-over', the freakish overthrows, the disputed decision, not to mention the fluctuations throughout the game – was incredible, an extraordinary climax to an excellent competition. As in almost every one of the Cup's forty-eight games, behaviour was excellent. The crowds loved the skills and dramas on show. Umpiring was good, pitches provided interesting cricket, and the outcome of the competition was open until the very last ball. The whole event, and in particular the final, provided fine publicity for the game.

Paul Ellis/Getty Images

New Zealand must take the greatest credit for this. They have led the world in sporting behaviour and attitudes. First their rugby team. When they changed coach and policy in 2008, they put at the top of their list of values not 'winning', or 'aggression', or even 'team spirit', but *humility*

– in particular the humility in being willing to face shortcomings and open to learning, especially after good performances. There is always room for improvement. Moreover, they adopted an approach in which the players themselves cleaned up their dressing room after matches, including after winning the World Cup in 2011. 'We made the mess, we clear it up,' was the message. They actively resisted the temptation to grandiosity and self-importance. They disclaimed any temptation that they were owed adoration, even service.

Moreover, even after the most physically gruelling matches, their captain and others were generous to the opposition, and modest about their own performance.

In cricket, New Zealand had reached the World Cup Final in 2015, in which Australia beat them in Melbourne. The occasion epitomised a radical difference between the attitudes of these two teams. In a radio interview after the game, Brad Haddin, Australia's wicketkeeper, said: 'They were that nice to us in New Zealand and we were that uncomfortable. I said in the team meeting: "I can't stand for this any more. We're going at them as hard as we can." I'm not playing cricket like this. If we get another crack at these guys in the final, I'm letting everything out.' In that final, several New Zealand players received 'hefty' verbal send-offs, the first two from Haddin.

Characteristically, Brendon McCullum was generous after the match (no doubt provoking Haddin even more). 'I think the focus should be more on how well Australia played and how they deserved this victory, rather than with any minor issues on the way through.'

But why should generosity make some opposition players uncomfortable? Why did Haddin find it intolerable? I don't know, but here are some possible reasons.

One is that the generosity is felt to be insincere and weak, perhaps hypocritical. Indeed, generosity may not be the main element in the story. I remember an incident at primary school when I was seven. The teacher, Mr Mee, was called to the door and spoke for several minutes to someone outside. The noise of us children became louder. When he came in, he picked on three of us, two boys from a local home for looked-after children, and me, and hit us round the head. Afterwards I remember tears coming to my eyes as I told my version of the story to others, saying that I didn't mind for myself, but how terrible for the boys from the Home. Even then I think I knew I was tearful because I was creating an image of myself as a martyr; I was moved by my own dramatised virtue of the event. I had a shrewd inkling that it was hypocritical.

Nevertheless, rising above insults or hurt need not be insincere. The New Zealand cricketers' ability to desist from instant retaliatory reactions to sledging, or McCullum's declining to make a fuss about it, may not have been a matter of standing on high moral ground. It may have become second nature, may have been genuinely noble. If so, perhaps Haddin and others were more like the playground gang hating those in their peer group at school who want to get on with the work and learn from teachers rather than bait them. If so, the Haddin reaction was probably a matter of converting their potential shame at their own boorishness into shamelessness; they may have been envious of those who could deal with loss more gracefully. The gang builds itself and its values up, projecting their unowned shame onto the opposition. They sneer at goodness so as not to lose face. On this reading, the Australian reaction was a mixture of envy, shame and contempt.

Haddin's response reminds me of the illiterate Athenian who, in 482 BCE, wished to cast his vote for an ostracism. This procedure offered a chance to the citizens to vote to exile one person for ten years, presumably to defuse internal political conflict. Offering to help the voter by writing the name of the man he wanted exiled on the *ostrakon* (the clay item that functioned as a voting slip), Aristides asked him whose name he should inscribe. The man told him: 'Aristides.' Asked why, the voter said he was fed up with hearing him referred to as 'the Just'. Aristides lived up to his name, writing his own name on the slip as requested. Three years later he was recalled to help lead the fight against the invading Persians – and later to act as an important negotiator for the city-state.

This was a case, it seems, of someone resenting a man's virtue, whether from envy or because of Aristides' presumed sense of superiority.

McCullum was, indeed, generous, non-retaliatory and genuinely modest. By his own account, he hadn't always been so. Becoming captain in 2012, he and coach Mike Hesson set about transforming the culture of the team after they had been bowled out for 45 by South Africa in the First Test in 2013. In an interview in June 2015, before a two-Test series in England, he said:

> Just because there is more at stake now doesn't mean you should lose the innocence of why you played the game in the first place. For a long time I had lost that, and I think our team had lost (it) . . . We expected the game to owe us something. We almost felt entitled because of the fact we were playing international cricket. There was no soul about our cricket . . . It sounds a bit corny, but we talk about the playful little boy who fell in love with the game. When you have that mindset you can be positive and aggressive, because you're thinking about what can go right rather than what might go wrong.

Jonathan Liew, McCullum's interviewer, writes of the 'real gift' of that New Zealand side being an 'ability to take success and failure with the same level-headed equanimity' – shades of Kipling's 'If'.

Moreover, learning perhaps from the Haddin experiences earlier that year, McCullum spoke about criticism: 'You're always going to be criticised to a degree. Some people didn't like Mother Teresa.'

McCullum's attitude echoes comments from earlier times. One

came from Keith Andrew, who kept wicket for Northants, and for England in two Tests: 'Being successful is one thing, but we want to enjoy our lives as well, and part of that is friendship between sportsmen.' And during the 1950s when a player in the Gloucestershire dressing room said 'It's a good feeling to win,' off-spinner 'Bomber' Wells recalls: 'Old Emmett [the captain, George Emmett] got up. "It's good to lose, too. It keeps your feet on the ground. You should never gloat over winning." He went on for ten minutes about playing in the right spirit. People . . . now don't realise how much he did for the county . . . He was magnificent.'

In contrast to Haddin, many players have responded positively to the McCullum type of attitude. The latter's good friend Eoin Morgan who had played with McCullum for Middlesex in 2016 and 2017, said before the final: 'He has taught me about leadership. He proved you can get to the highest level by being yourselves. He has quite a bit to do with our improvement. The way New Zealand played in 2015 [against England] proved you can get to the top by being yourselves, not by being a novelty.'

Quoting the cautious approach in England's recent defeat against Sri Lanka in the 2019 World Cup as the example where this anxious failure to trust their usual approach had contributed to their loss, Morgan added: 'Our biggest risk during the World Cup was not staying true to what we believe.' He also spoke about the importance of diversity: 'Players were in new territory playing in a final at Lord's. Each person has to respond in his own way. We don't have to be the same. England had the rub of the green on the day. Adil Rashid said it his way: "Allah was on our side today."'

When asked what he had to do before the Super-over he spoke about trying to help people relax and smile. Another tribute, perhaps, to McCullum.

And regarding the overthrows, Morgan said: 'It's not something that you cheer or celebrate. That could have been you.'

5

GOATS

'You do the batting, Mike, we'll do the appealing, and leave the umpiring to the umpire.'

Ian Chappell, Australian cricketer

Spirit-of-cricket goats come in different guises. Players (and occasionally others, for instance umpires) may indulge in criminality – match-fixing or even, rarely, violence. They may be dishonest – for example, claiming catches when they know the ball has bounced. They may show up umpires by dissent, petulantly snatching their cap at the end of an over. Trickery is itself a tricky subject, sometimes involving skill and ingenuity, but sometimes too underhand, worryingly deceptive. There is also negativity, a crushing of life; the opposite of positive cricket.

(Though I feel sorry for the goat. Some of us need to be a bit cantankerous and independent, a bit goatish; less ovine, less liable to go astray in blunderingly following the flock.)

If a batsman chases an opponent and hits him with his bat, or attempts to do so, he is breaking the law of the land. He is guilty of assault or attempted assault. There is no need for cricket's Laws to mention this; the prohibition on violence applies in any area of life. (Though it may be right for cricket to institute instantaneous penalties within the game for such egregious behaviour.)

Cricketers may break the law while away from the game. Cricketers have been charged for brawling, drink-driving, domestic violence, murder, rape, drug-smuggling, fraud and so on. Being subject to separate hearings and penalties at the hands of cricket authorities, clubs or employers, they may also be open to double penalties; they bring the game into disrepute. All this seems clear and appropriate, though of course painful and troubling.

Do cricketers in high-profile cases get preferential treatment? It may even be felt that they *should*, since they suffer this double jeopardy. Alternatively, as examples to the youth, should test players and other stars be held to higher standards than others? Is it fair to expect them to be role models? My answer is that, as far as possible, they should be treated exactly like anyone else. This is also a feature of the 'rule of law' – that no one, not even the monarch, is above the law.

Certainly, more is demanded. Learie Constantine, a budding star in Trinidad, hurt himself while playing football. C. L. R. James writes:

> Wilton St Hill of Shannon [a club side in Trinidad] met me and said: 'You heard! Learie is injured playing football. That fool!

What right has a man like Constantine to be playing football, you tell me?' He was terribly angry. All of us were looking to him to do great things.

Constantine had a role as a representative, and as such his supporters required more of him than of others.

Prominent sportsmen are bound to get greater exposure than others for their faults and crimes; they often are more provoked, too. Notoriously, Diego Maradona scored a goal against England with his fist, and got away with it. But anyone who has seen Asif Kapadia's 2019 film about his football career will have no doubt about the extreme adulation, abuse and temptation he was subjected to – all amounting to a corrupting environment. Hemmed in, packaged, adored, hated, he was the recipient of constant inducement – to passivity, drug use, and then to blackmail.

None of this excuses, but it is part of the explanation.

Non-criminal violence happens on the field too, as part of the game. Attempts to hurt the batsman, whether by persistent use of short-pitched bowling when the batsman is not up to defending himself, or by a fielder deliberately throwing the ball at the batsman, are against the Laws of cricket, and the umpire is obliged to act (many don't). Forbidden too is the bowling of a beamer, that is, a fast, high, full toss (now outlawed), which may well not be picked up even by a fine, well-set batsman, in good light. None of this precludes the bowling of bouncers, aimed at the chest or head. The purpose of this is to get the batsman out, whether fending the ball off and being caught off his glove or the shoulder of the bat, or caught out hooking. Further, the threat of such a delivery puts the batsman on the back foot, literally and metaphorically, thus making the pitched-up delivery more likely to get him out and less likely to be scored off. Most sport involves a risk of injury, and cricket is no different. The difficulty lies in drawing the line between fair and unfair uses of bouncers.

Was bodyline (Douglas Jardine's strategy in 1932–3) a form of attack that justified Australian captain Bill Woodfull's assertion at Adelaide: 'There are two sides out there and only one is playing cricket'?

I am conflicted about bodyline. Like Greg Chappell, I have a sneaking regard for what Jardine did, but I still in the end feel that it went too far, that in an era when there was little provision for limiting persistently dangerous bowling, his tactic was too ruthless. Moreover, bodyline was employed before there was a limitation on fielders behind square on the leg side (now, only two are allowed). All this meant that such bowling, especially with Jardine's field-placings and with the then current attitude to wides, made proper cricket strokes more or less impossible. So, was bodyline against the spirit of cricket? I think so.

Certain forms of corruption may break the law of the land, as well as the Laws and the spirit of the game. A typical case is spot-fixing, where a bowler deliberately concedes a minimum number of runs within a specific number of balls or overs, or a batsman ensures that no more than a certain number of runs are scored in a nominated period. The player gets paid, usually by a corrupt bookmaker, for giving this information and then ensuring the outcome. Such activities are, at least in some countries, illegal. Going against the whole point of the sporting activity, defrauding spectators, team-mates and opposition alike, they are also deeply repugnant to honest cricketers and spectators.

A brief comment here about sledging, mental disintegration and some forms of racism. Words, gestures and gait are not only the expression of ideas or emotions, they may also be performative utterances. They have an impact on others, and are consciously or unconsciously meant to do so. They are, my friend Shekhar Kamat once said, akin to perfumes and smells – they get through to others, permeating their personal skins. On a cricket field such attitudes are not only expressions of confidence and arrogance, they are also, like hate crimes, *actions* aimed to arouse apprehension and self-doubt in others. Here I mention them for the sake of completeness.

Cheating, which is against the spirit, is also against the Laws of cricket, or against the playing conditions for a competition.

Here are some examples. Just as a golfer may surreptitiously alter the lie of the ball to gain an advantage, so a cricketer may break the rules to improve his own, or his side's, chances. Time-wasting is a case in point. Some require *mens rea*, that is, they depend on intentions and states of mind; as a result, they are often hard for umpires to judge and to enforce.

It's not just the players who owe respect to the spirit of cricket. Umpires have been found guilty of making biased decisions in exchange for financial favours. Towards the end of the era of home umpires, Pakistan and India both complained about English umpire David Constant, and England complained about certain Indian and Pakistan umpires. The arguments climaxed when England captain Mike Gatting wagged his finger in the face of Pakistan umpire Shakoor Rana at Faisalabad in 1987. Gatting felt that the umpire had been unjust in alleging that he had moved a fielder.

A West Indian player told me that not long after Imran Khan (later elected, partly as a result of his campaign against corruption in politics, to be the country's prime minister) was first made captain of Pakistan, he was asked by a Pakistani umpire which opposition batsman he would particularly like to have 'eliminated'. The umpire offered Imran services like a Mafia hitman to a putative Godfather. Imran was appalled by this flat contradiction of the spirit of fair play, and refused point-blank to have anything to do with the offer.

Furthermore, he not only argued forcibly for neutral umpires in international cricket (a practice not put into action formally until a decade later) but was also responsible for the invitation to two Indian umpires to stand in a Test against West Indies at Lahore in 1986. In 1989–90 he arranged for two English umpires, John Hampshire and John Holder, to stand in all four Tests against India. Here is an example of the spirit of cricket; Imran was willing to cede possible favours to his own team in the interests of fair play. He was willing to be proactive in promoting what became mandatory.

As for reprobate umpires: a much less serious situation occurs when an umpire is carried away from his neutral stance by excitement or partisanship, or indeed by unconscious bias of one kind or another. I was once given out caught behind off my pad strap in Lahore. That evening, the umpire sent me a message via the liaison officer: 'I am very sorry about that decision. I felt my arm going up and couldn't stop it.' Giving me out was a spontaneous act that bypassed his reflective mind, so it was more than simply a mistake. Like a sheep, he followed the flock, carried away by forty thousand people appealing. His decision-making fell short of what we might call the spirit of umpiring, which includes leaving room for reflection on first impressions and requires a repudiation of all partisan feelings or crowd pressures. But his sending of the message, an expression of regret and apology, was an instance of a good spirit. The charming naivety of the gesture disarmed me and softened my resentment.

To go back to players. It is against the spirit of the game to claim a catch when you know the ball has bounced. Traditionally, when a fielder knew he had not caught the ball cleanly, he would say so, and the batsman would stay. If the fielder indicated that he wasn't sure, the umpire would almost always give the benefit of the doubt to the batsman (rightly, as in other decision-making).

In the Test match in Lahore, in 1977, England off-spinner Geoff Cope took two wickets in two balls. The next was edged to me at slip. I was fairly sure that the ball had touched the ground, so disclaimed the catch. Despite the fact that this deprived Cope of a hat-trick, a feat that would have gone in the record books, my reaction was automatic. What I did was par for the course – most cricketers would have done the same. My reaction was almost, we might say, unthinking.

On another occasion, in a county match at Leicester, I dived forward at extra cover to catch a drive from Peter Marner. I was sure I'd caught it cleanly, and held the ball up. To my consternation, my team-mate Mike (M. J.) Smith, fielding alongside me at cover, was shouting: 'No, it bounced.' Naturally the umpire indicated not out. I was furious, but I managed (when I cooled down) to acknowledge that there are rare occasions when the fielder is genuinely but wrongly convinced that a catch is fair. (Similarly, though in the vast majority of cases batsmen know whether or not they have edged the ball, the bat being an extension of the body via the hands, there are rare occasions when they get it wrong, or are genuinely unsure.)

Recently, with the advent of cameras at high-level games, habits have changed. Fielders are less likely to declare a doubt, preferring to leave the decision to the umpires and the cameras. For some years technology has been used to adjudicate on such situations, with on-field umpires calling for assistance from the third umpire, who has access to clips of the event from different camera angles. A recent innovation has been for the on-field umpires to give a 'soft' signal – 'out' or 'not out' – to their off-field colleague who is monitoring the screen. The latter has to have convincing evidence of a mistake in order to overturn the soft signal, whichever it may be. I like this new procedure. It seems to me that cameras often foreshorten the scene depicted, which tends to make genuine catches look doubtful. This is one reason why batsmen stand rather than accept the fielder's word. The 'soft signal' rightly reflects the fact that the on-field umpires are in the best place for influencing, if not for definitively making, this kind of decision.

I learned recently that Ricky Ponting, who captained Australia's Test side from 2004 to 2011, used routinely to ask opposition captains before a series started if they would be willing to come to an agreement to take the fielder's word for these low 'catches' rather than relying on umpires and often misleading images from technology. According to Mike Atherton, the responses were 'usually' negative. I think Ponting was right, his opposite numbers wrong – in respect both of the facts and of his willingness to take a risk in mutual trust.

Interestingly, while it is against the spirit of cricket to claim a catch when one knows it is not out, it is not (in many circles) considered unsporting for the batsman to wait for the umpire's decision on whether he is out caught when he knows he has hit the ball. What could be the grounds for such a disparity? I suspect that it has to do with the fact that in the latter case the umpire has been appealed to, and it is, both in Law and in practice, up to him to come to a decision. Richard Hutton, who advocated walking, adds: 'Appealing is central to the whole argument. In appealing the bowler is invoking the judgement of the umpire, not that of the batsman. So, the batsman has a right to wait for the decision.'

I agree. The batsman is like the defendant in the dock, who does not have to plead (guilty or not guilty) or give evidence. He is entitled to wait. If he takes this course, the relevant moral issue is whether he accepts the decision in good grace, or whether he shows the umpire up by his body expression, or by frank dissent. Whereas the fielder who claims a catch that he knows to have been invalid sets going a quasi-judicial process; he is like a man initiating charges that he knows to be false, rather than someone who knows he is guilty declining to incriminate himself.

I would add that in my view it is against the spirit of cricket to appeal vehemently when you know the batsman is not out (for instance, the ball has pitched outside leg stump and as keeper you know this). Rod Marsh tells me that he followed this as a rule. 'But', he writes:

If you know a batsman has nicked one to you the keeper and has not been given out, do you then appeal for lbw next ball even if you know it has pitched just outside leg? Of course I'm talking pre-reviews – I say yes to the appeal. I think part of the game is being able to read the umpire's personality and as he is probably aware he made a mistake the previous ball then he is very likely to give him out second time around. This may be hard but to me is certainly fair. Having said that, under normal circumstances I wouldn't appeal if I knew the ball had pitched outside leg stump. This could be called gamesmanship and then we have to ask: is there room for gamesmanship in the game? Yes, in my opinion, sometimes there is.

I find this true to human nature, even if what this approach means is that one asks an umpire to 'correct' one wrong decision by making another.

One disadvantage of 'walking' is that there are some who choose their moment to walk or to stay. They are not consistent. They may walk less readily on 0 or 99, than on, say, 38 or 105. In cultures with a tradition of 'walking', fielding sides will feel aggrieved if they are convinced that the batsman hit the ball but didn't walk. Accusations of dishonesty arise; teams retaliate, there is a tendency for the whole atmosphere of a game to deteriorate. Everyone becomes childish, claiming in effect that 'it wasn't me who retaliated first'.

I confess that I did not always walk, even in county cricket. I still blush to remember these occasions. I remember a match at Dover, when I got a thin edge, which was caught by Alan Knott. I didn't walk. Umpire Alan Whitehead – a man I respect for his honesty and for treating all alike whatever their prestige or rank in the game – gave me out. I even looked him in the eye as I walked out, in a way that might have been interpreted as meaning that he had made a mistake. Thirty-five or so years later I met him at a talk I gave in Wells, Somerset, and apologised for this. As it turned out, he could not remember. But the shame I felt afterwards, even decades later, is a measure of the power of this culture, and of the discomfort we feel at our dishonourable behaviour.

On another occasion when I was at Cambridge, batting against that fine off-spinner, Don Shepherd of Glamorgan, I got my bat and pads tangled up together; the ball looped up to slip, and the Glamorgan team celebrated. I started to walk off. But at once I realised I was completely unsure whether or not I had hit the ball. By now, however, there was nothing for it, I had to keep going. It can take courage to stand.

There are also situations where the fielding side don't believe you hit the ball, and even apologise instantly for their aborted appeal. This happened to me once in Pakistan. Trying to late-cut a spinner, the ball touched my glove as it went through to Wasim Bari. There was an almost simultaneous noise as my bat hit the ground. Bari quickly checked his appeal and apologised, the umpire shook his head vigorously. I did not walk.

Ted Dexter, one of the proponents of the Preamble within the Laws of Cricket document in 2000, now believes that walking 'led to more trouble than it was worth . . . Better to wait for the umpire. The slightest move to influence the umpires' decision – e.g. shaking the head, looking at the edge of the bat – should be penalised.'

Australian cricketer John Inverarity agrees citing his father, Mervyn, ('a scrupulously fair man'), who advised, 'Leave it to the umpire. You will get many bad decisions [how true!] and many fortunate reprieves. When the umpire gives you out, put your head up and walk briskly to the pavilion.'

One reason I have always supported DRS is that its presence improves behaviour, since more often than not, batsmen now do walk (even if largely for pragmatic rather than for moral reasons), and even if they don't, the review almost always makes clear what the truth of the matter was.

* * *

During the decade or so when the Board of Control for Cricket in India (BCCI) refused to join with other countries in adopting the DRS in international cricket, one of their main arguments was that giving players the right to review a decision went against the principle of the finality of the umpire's ruling.

I agree with BCCI that part of the spirit of the game is indeed to accept decisions without dissent; when given out, the batsman should walk off without displaying a sense of injustice; when the decision is not out, bowlers and fielders should not make a fuss; they should get on with the game. (The one Major League baseball game I saw live during my year in California in the late 1960s, between the Los Angeles Dodgers and the Washington Senators, was held up for several minutes by a brawl between ten or more players over an alleged 'illegal spit-ball', the umpires trying vigorously but vainly to unglue them).

Nevertheless, one could incorporate BCCI's point by rewording the maxim as: 'The players are required to accept the decision of the umpires once legitimate means of questioning it have been exhausted.' My view was, and is, that the value of avoiding mistakes, of getting closer to the truth, outweighs BCCI's qualms. As in tennis, challenging the umpire's call in this way is not, or certainly need not be, disrespectful.

In the World Cup semi-final against Australia, Jason Roy was understandably but incorrectly given out caught behind off the bowling of Mitchell Starc. There were no reviews left, as his opening partner Jonny Bairstow, when given out lbw, had used up the single failed review permitted. Roy, who had batted brilliantly, did not move from his crease. He was at first nonplussed, then clearly outraged. Touchingly, umpire Marais Erasmus, who was standing at square leg, came up to him, put his arm round his shoulder and quietly escorted him down the pitch towards the pavilion. Erasmus, going beyond the call of duty into the realm of care, behaved in accordance with

75

the spirit of cricket; Roy, acting as if he was the first person in the history of the game to suffer the disappointment of a wrong decision, did not.

* * *

Trickiness ranges from the decidedly dodgy to the admirably shrewd. Sleight of hand and eye occur both as fair play and foul. A trickster is a con man. But a leg-spinner with a bag of tricks is clever. His deceptions are well disguised and skilful.

Bluff and double bluff are central to sport. Maradona would feint to the left, wrong-foot the defender, and go right. Googlies look like leg breaks but are in fact off breaks, and turn the other way. One aim of captain and fast bowler is to get it into the batsman's head that a bouncer is coming so that he is less able to get forward to the well pitched-up ball.

Batsmen and bowler constantly second-guess each other. In short forms of the game, where run opportunities have to be manu-factured by the batsman, shrewd guesswork, reading hints from the bowler's whole approach, and boldness are vital. Having committed to, say, moving outside the off stump in the moment of delivery, he often has to keep his head still and trust his eye even when his premeditation turns out to be wrong. One of the best of current batsmen, AB de Villiers, manages to do this supremely well. I'm also reminded of Knott's ability to play the sweep to almost any ball bowled by a spinner. What's crucial, he said, is keeping the head still, not trying to hit the ball too hard and watching it all the way.

I recall decades ago hearing a possibly apocryphal story (uncon-firmed by people I talked to about him) told to counter any idea that Revd David Sheppard lacked toughness as a captain. The suggestion was that, when standing up to the stumps, the wicketkeeper in his team, having taken the ball down the leg side, turned sharply round as if he'd missed it; at the same time, slip and short leg ran towards fine leg. The striker set off for a run and was smartly run out. Whether it was true of David or not, it poses an interesting thought-experiment. What would we think of such a scheme?

I feel uneasy about it. The ploy smacks of the wrong kind of trickery. It reminds me of Ashwin's running out of Buttler, where the fraction of a second's delay shifted the event into the realm of entrapment. In the 'Sheppard' case too, there was a similar entrapment of the batsman. He was lured into running. The ploy would have had to be planned, even rehearsed – one element that made what the Australians did with the sandpaper more culpable.

Vintcent van der Bijl, the giant South African fast bowler with whom I played a season for Middlesex in 1980 and who is a good friend to this day, reports in his autobiography *Cricket in the Shadows* an incident that he feels embarrassed about. Crucial to this event was also a brief delay.

Van der Bijl writes that he felt his success at Middlesex in 1980 contributed to his becoming 'more confident and possibly even arrogant'. Enlarging on this background, he reports that he had become more cantankerous towards umpires and opposition batsmen, and that his 'chirping' had become more personal.

The incident itself occurred when he was bowling for Natal in a Cup Final against Western Province in 1982. Allan Lamb was the non-striking batsman:

> The other batsman, Adrian Kuiper, played the ball down the leg side of the pitch. I fielded it at silly mid-on and, turning to go back to my mark, saw that Lamb, backing up, had yet to regain his crease. I threw down the wicket and Lamb, still out of his ground, was run out . . .
>
> What worried me when I saw the TV replay a week later was that I took two steps back towards my bowling mark before

throwing at the wicket . . . At the time, unaware of the delay, I thought the run-out was acceptable and in the spirit of the game, but it was wrong . . . I am beginning to believe that the ball was dead once I had taken those two steps back . . . and that Lamb should not have been given out.

I would add two thoughts of my own. The first is that 'Vince' was in my experience a person who played entirely within the spirit of the game, exuding fun and friendliness alongside a fierce competitiveness. The second is that in that last opinion (that Lamb should not have been given out as the ball was dead), he brings together (as with Ashwin, and in the M. J. K. Smith 'run-out' at Johannesburg) the spirit and the Law. He states that the ball should have been regarded as dead. But he also goes on to say that whatever the Law implied, his action, though it felt spontaneous, was unconsciously driven by a momentary opportunism that was not direct and honourable. He speaks of a 'new competitiveness, a hidden killer instinct', that had 'suddenly surfaced'.

I also believe that it is part of his generosity and open-mindedness to realise this, to apologise publicly after the event, and to write the account so honestly in his book, all of which is the expression of a good spirit, both the spirit of cricket and the spirit of life.

In 1980, I put all ten fielders, including wicketkeeper David Bairstow, on the boundary for the last ball of a One Day International against West Indies in Sydney, when the latter needed three runs to win. We won by two runs. In the instant of making my decision, I'd remembered M. J. K. Smith doing the same thing to win a Sunday League match for Warwickshire at Lord's a year or two before. In Sydney, wicketkeeper David Bairstow had a refilled beer can thrown at him from the crowd, and I received metaphorical beer cans.

Twelve months before, in a Test match on the same ground, I put seven men on the leg side for our off-spinners, Geoff Miller and

John Emburey. Some Australians were highly critical, accusing me of negative and defensive tactics, despite the fact that we had three or four close (attacking) catchers and dismissed Australia for 111 in 40 overs. I regarded their huffy anger as an expression of sour grapes, related to historic controversies and resentments.

I would still defend these two experiments in field-placing, which some observers thought went against the spirit of cricket. Leg-side bowling has at times been used in a cynical way to preclude proper cricket strokes. Wicketkeepers can have backstops but (one might feel) should not be reduced to becoming gloved backstops themselves. I would counter: who says a wicketkeeper can't be a backstop?

More relevantly, neither ruse deviously ruled out the potential for skilful, powerful or lucky batting. In one case, putting the 'keeper on the boundary didn't preclude the batsman hitting the ball for four or six. It just made it less likely that this would happen from an edge or a leg bye. With regard to 7–2 leg-side fields, it takes skill to bowl off-spinners with such a field. Miller and Emburey were not bowling at the pads. The field I set was an invitation to batsmen to take risks by hitting against the spin into the vacant off side. (I admit that the predictability of the reaction gave spice to my pleasure in the whole episode.)

The reaction itself emerged, I believe, from an unthinking assumption that packing the leg side in this way was no different from earlier strategies used by England in the Ashes series; first as an essential element of bodyline, second when in 1953 Trevor Bailey, possibly bowling to instructions from captain Len Hutton, bowled wide of the leg stump to restrict Australia in their run-chase at Headingley.

Perhaps I can highlight this by contrasting it with a different case. In 1981 at Melbourne, when New Zealand needed 6 off the last ball to tie the match, Greg Chappell instructed his younger brother Trevor to roll the ball along the ground under-arm. Rod Marsh was heard to call out: 'No, Greg, no, you can't do that.' Chappell was unwell during this match. Exhausted and stressed, he'd wanted to leave the field earlier that afternoon but was dissuaded by Marsh. In Chappell's words: 'I wasn't fit. I mean, I was mentally wrung out, I was physically wrung out, and I was fed up with the whole system . . . I suppose I felt things were closing in on me, and it was a cry for help . . . I didn't recognise how far down I was . . . I was disappointed that there was nobody else either within the playing group or within the administration who seemed to understand.'

Almost forty years on, I still feel uneasy about what Chappell did. The quote shows that he too feels uneasy. But I'm not sure I can put my finger on why it still strikes me as significantly different from my two actions. I *think* it relates to Chappell's resorting to a ploy that ruled out what would have been a remarkable piece of skill by the batsman. Instead of the hitting of a six being made difficult and extremely unlikely, it was rendered out of the question.

At the same time, I'm aware that rolling the ball under-arm was at the time legal, and that it was not unlike what any current rugby side would do when, leading narrowly in an international, and having kept possession for the last few minutes of the game, they kick the ball into touch the moment the clock has run down. The pundits don't criticise this; nor do I. To do so would be redolent of the mentality of the Edwardian-era amateur soccer team, the Corinthian Casuals, who I'm told deliberately missed penalties because they scorned to score so easily as a result of what may have been a trivial offence. Yet many, including the later Chappell himself, would frown at the cricketing ploy.

As an aside: mention of the Corinthian Casuals reminds me of a story about the person whom the lecture that set this book idea going is named after: Colin Cowdrey. In 1974, at the age of forty-one, Cowdrey heroically accepted an invitation to go from the depths of an English winter to Perth, to face Dennis Lillee and Jeff Thomson in their pomp on the fastest Test pitch in the world. The version of the story I prefer is that on his way in to bat he went up to Thomson, who was waiting at the end of his run, shook his hand, and said: 'Mr Thomson, I presume. My name is Cowdrey. Very pleased to meet you.'

I gather from Colin's son Jeremy that the story is true, or at least close enough to be true in spirit!

6

MEANINGLESS GUFF?

'The Spirit of Cricket is a mysterious entity. Until recently, it lived with the Tooth Fairy, Zeus, the Will-o'-the-Wisp and the ghost of W. G. Grace in an imaginary cloud castle that, depending on the prevailing wind, is located three or four miles above the Lord's Pavilion.'

Andrew Hughes

One outcome of the 'Mankading' debate was the questioning in some quarters of the whole notion of the spirit of cricket, as if *it* were responsible for the dispute. The writer Andrew Hughes described this 'nebulous' aspiration as a 'will-o'-the-wisp, located in an imaginary cloud castle three or four miles above the Lord's Pavilion'. Mike Atherton referred to it (in 2016) as 'a lot of meaningless guff'.

So: is it a matter of 'motherhood and apple pie' – too vague, too worthy to be relevant, too good to be true? Some criticised the presence of the Spirit of Cricket as a Preamble to the Laws, claiming that it would be of value only if it were to be accommodated – with precision – *within* the Laws. And is it, moreover, a disguised expression of cultural, social or colonial oppression, liable to be biased in favour of the powerful and the privileged?

I too used to question the notion of the spirit of cricket. I was worried that it was indeed nebulous, and I felt that those who advocated it most strongly tended to sound (or even be) patronising or pompous. 'Spirit' was sometimes used to support a set of standards that were proclaimed most loudly as part of a Victorian ethos, but not always lived out consistently on the cricket field, let alone in other walks of life. One vice attributed to the English was hypocrisy; 'perfidious Albion' was how we were regarded in some parts of the world.

I am reminded of the Marquess of Queensberry, who in 1867 lent his aristocratic name to the new codified rules for boxing, which turned a licensed punch-up into a more or less respectable sport, but who almost thirty years later hounded Oscar Wilde to disgrace, prison, and an early death.

A small but rich example of English superiority was evinced when one of England's best-ever captains, Ray Illingworth, was disparagingly described by writer E. W. Swanton – 'the biggest snob in English cricket', according to Doug Insole – as 'Sergeant' Illingworth.

But I have changed my mind. I now maintain that the Preamble *rightly* leaves a lot vague. There is often room for dispute and personal construction with regard to what constitutes respect, or fairness or hardness of play, or proper spirit. None of these qualities can be laid down in concrete ways. Much depends on good nature and orientation – things said humorously may be acceptable, while the same words animated by malice and venom inhabit a different moral universe. A relationship in which there are lively altercations and occasional rows is a world apart from one frozen in contempt and indifference. There is a difference between a captain who is aloof and superior, and one who is passionate while maintaining a proper detachment; one is scorned, the other respected and readily followed.

The emphasis in the current Preamble on 'respect', though correct, makes me uncomfortable: respect after all has to be earned (by captains, administrators, umpires and others). It is right to respect these roles, positions and status, to give people occupying them the benefit of the doubt, at least to start with. But I think there is a danger that this emphasis encourages too much deference and the following of orders, as opposed to challenge, questioning and telling truth to power. Many of the 'traditions of the game' – a phrase deliberately omitted from the 2017 version of the Preamble – are not worthy of respect; nowadays, we do not, for example, respect the prejudices underlying the distinction between 'Gentlemen' and 'Players', nor the exclusion of women from membership of MCC until 1998.

There are, I suggest, two bases for authority, embedded in two types of leadership. One works best when the end is clear-cut and known in advance, so that what is called for is clear knowledge of ends and of the means to these ends, combined with clear instructions to subordinates. Here experts are in a strong position to formulate and direct strategy. This style or type of leadership has been called 'technical leadership'. On the cricket field a captain may sometimes be right to set a particular field and expect the bowler to bowl to that field in a disciplined way. Illingworth once told me a story from his days captaining Yorkshire. Playing Somerset in a limited-overs game, Illingworth decided that their best plan against the great attacking batsman, Viv Richards, was to bowl outside his off stump when he first came in to bat. If he hit these balls through the leg side he had to take some risk; and they could defend the off side. The bowler was Graham Stevenson. His first four balls to Richards all went for fours through the vacant square leg area. When Illingworth remonstrated with him, he said: 'I just had the idea I'd get him out if I bowled at leg stump.'

In this first form of leadership, the main attitude asked of those who are led is doing what they're told to do as well as they can. This may be to go all out for an improbable win, or to play defensively for a draw – or indeed to bowl outside off stump. But if taken to an extreme, this kind of leadership style invites people to follow orders blindly, without questioning.

The second type of leadership, sometimes called 'adaptive leadership', comes from a different set of assumptions. This deeper leadership task is to develop followers who are also capable of leading. It values independent thinking.

In this mode, there is no measurable or definite target or plan; instead there is an open-ended, longer-term aim of fostering creativity and an ability to think outside the box. Such a process calls for different qualities and attitudes in both the 'leader' or mentor and in his or her team or group. As captain, I wanted all the members of a cricket team to think like captains, not only about their individual skills or specialities, but also about the whole game. I think I was going even further; I was trying to develop the person as well as his thinking. Steve Waugh described his job as captain of Australia as helping players become not only better players, but better, fuller people. This broad project led to a variety of initiatives, including stopping off en route to England at Gallipoli, where many young Australians had died in the First World War, and having meetings at which players would read out loud their own writing or that of others.

The same goes for the input from parents and teachers. In some contexts, these adults know what their charges need, and may rightly tell them what is required, expecting to be obeyed. ('Never step into the road until I say so,' for example, when said to a three-year-old.) But their broader aim is to help those in their care to mature in their thinking and behaviour, to consider the facts, take responsibility, respect other people's wishes as well as their own; and be open to surprises.

The good leader in this second mode does a lot of listening. Asked how as a leader you gain respect and a reputation for listening to people, I responded: 'A good start is to do it – to really respect the team (as people with a right to their own views), to actually listen to them!' Sometimes the best leadership involves not telling, not speaking as if one knows, not assuming there is a knowable route to a preferred end. There is a story told about a psychiatrist and psychoanalyst called Dr Tom Main. He was the director of an innovative mental hospital, the Cassel, back in the 1950s and '60s. One day a junior doctor, in panic, asked what he should do with a particularly difficult and frightening patient. Main was quiet for a few moments. Then he said: 'Don't just *do* something: stand there.'

As in a good team, a lively family doesn't agree all the time. The children are not passive. There is no steep hierarchy. And in democratic societies we agree to sacrifice some of the security that comes from knowing our place and unquestioningly accepting instructions for the freedom to disagree, argue and make our own mistakes. We need to learn to lead ourselves as much as lead others. Moreover, no one can know where the next good idea is going to come from. Nor can we know who will be called upon to take the lead in a crisis.

Dictators, by contrast, whether of the left or the right, favour dogma over freedom, control over controversy, discipline over debate. They themselves become the sole arbiters of what is permissible or 'right'. Instead of encouraging independence of mind they enforce obedience. They argue that ordinary people prefer to have values made absolutely clear, and only understand harsh discipline. According to them, the man and woman in the street are not up to the freedom of making up their minds for themselves, let alone to an ability to choose and stick to the right course. This method often prioritises the carrot and the stick over rationality.

Leadership specialist Ronald Heifetz wrote: 'Leadership should generate capacity, not dependency . . . The need for leadership today is less that we know, and more that collectively we have the courage to learn.'

This is close to what the poet John Keats wrote about 'negative capability'. 'That is,' he said, 'when a man is capable of being in uncertainties, mysteries, doubts, without any irritable reaching after fact and reason.' We need to be able to refrain from quick fixes. Keats also suggested that, in order to grow as people, as selves, as 'souls', we need to face up to the inevitability of failure and disappointment; of suffering.

As we saw with New Zealand sportspeople, confidence includes the deeper willingness to not-know, to be ready to learn, to use success as well as failure for further improvements.

Is this New Zealand attitude too much to expect? Are we wrong to ask people to grow? Should we settle for a more mundane happiness or contentedness? Is it a myth to aspire to an elevated version of the spirit of cricket, just as it is undoubtedly too much for some people to live up to the vows of celibacy and selflessness required of priests? And the ethical expectation of abstinence and reflectiveness with patients asks a lot of psychoanalysts.

In his novel *The Brothers Karamazov*, Dostoyevsky presents a story within a story. Jesus returns to earth, arriving in Seville on a day when one hundred 'heretics' are being burned to death at the stake. He performs some miracles and is recognised by the people. However, he is seen as a threat by the powers-that-be, is promptly arrested and then sentenced to be burned to death the next day.

The Grand Inquisitor visits him in his cell to defend the attitudes of the Church of that time and place. He argues that freedom – as offered and advocated by Christ, and especially the freedom to choose between good and evil – is too difficult for most people. The Church, he says, has accepted what Christ failed to accept, that obedience simplifies life, enabling the acquisition of basic necessities, the transfer of responsibility to the leaders of the Church, and salvation from both failure and sin. The Inquisitor says to Christ: 'Respecting him [the common man] less, you would have demanded less of him, and that would be closer to love, for his burden would be lighter.'

The burden of knowledge and freedom is borne on behalf of the generality of the populace by the Church leaders, by the Inquisitors and Popes who, like the elites of Marxist–Leninist regimes four or five centuries later, took on the responsibility of decision-making. They themselves, the Inquisitor suggests, suffer from having to lie and deceive the people, while the 'feeble will become timid, look to us, and cling to us in fear, like chicks to a hen'. In arriving at this conclusion, the Inquisitor himself lost his own faith. He had by now no belief in God. As a younger believer:

> He himself ate roots in the desert and raved, overcoming his flesh, in order to make himself free and perfect, but still loved mankind all his life, and suddenly opened his eyes and saw that there is no great moral blessedness in achieving perfection of the will only to become convinced at the same time that millions of the rest of God's creatures have been set up only for mockery, that they will never be strong enough to manage their freedom, that it was not for such geese that the great idealist had his dream of harmony.

The arguments informing his present stance are presented by Dostoyevsky as Satan's whisper in his ear; as 'the directives of the intelligent spirit [the Devil who tempted Christ in the wilderness], and to that end [lured him] to accept lies and deceit, and lead people, consciously now, to death and destruction, deceiving them, moreover, all along the way, so that they somehow do not notice where they are being led, so that . . these pitiful blind men consider themselves happy.'

In Dostoyevsky's story, Jesus says nothing, but listens carefully. When the Inquisitor has finished, he (Jesus) 'gently kisses him on his bloodless, ninety-year-old lips'.

The idea that love and freedom are too burdensome for ordinary humans and should therefore be refused admission is radically opposed to the stance of many Christian leaders in the history of the Church. It's also opposed to that of psychoanalysis, one of whose core values is that facing reality and truth is better (to the extent that one can begin to bear it, and provided we can find help to do so) than living in either an illusory or an utterly controlled world. *All things being equal*, it's better to own one's own feelings freely, and take responsibility for one's actions and orientations, than simply to follow authority, sheep-like.

Nevertheless, facing the facts and taking responsibility for our choices is hard. It is at best an aspiration. At times we all need to resort to denial of painful feelings like loss or disappointment. We need escape routes.

We all have different ways of denying reality, whether temporarily or permanently.

One challenge offered by sport is the requirement to face both victory and defeat, success and failure, those 'twin impostors' as Kipling put it, without too much triumphalism or complacency on one side, without too much desolation, resentment or surrender on the other.

＊　＊　＊

Today, the remit and atmosphere of MCC have changed radically. This private club, that once held sway over cricket throughout the Empire, now has a role in the sport somewhat akin to that of the House of Lords in politics; both bodies lack power but retain residual influence. As such, MCC is still the custodian of the Laws of Cricket. It runs a respected World Cricket Committee. It can be part of the 'conscience of the game' (as South African cricketer Shaun Pollock said), without setting itself up on a pinnacle of moral rectitude.

In the UK we have been forced to admit, reluctantly, that institutional – and largely unconscious – prejudice, whether on grounds of wealth, race, gender or religion, persists. I am sure that class consciousness is a factor on both sides. ('Of course, you must have a private income, Mike, to become captain of Middlesex' – committee member to me in 1971. And: 'Don't think you're so clever, Brearley, just because you wear socks' – spectator at Headingley, Leeds, in the same year.)

We might even ask if cricket is becoming a game of the 'haves'. It is played in fewer and fewer schools, and never shown live on terrestrial TV. I think this is a real worry for the future.

Having said all this, I don't believe I speak only from an Establishment point of view. People at all levels express strong values in how they play and view the game. Every sport (and organised social activity) has its largely unwritten codes. In some cases, aspects of these codes are adumbrated in words. The Rules of golf used to begin with guidance on behaviour headed by the word 'Etiquette'. This has now been re-titled as a 'Preamble'. The first instruction to golfers is: 'Play the course as you find it and the ball as it lies.' The second: 'Play by the rules and in the spirit of the game.' And third: 'You are responsible for applying your own penalties if you breach a Rule, so that you cannot gain any potential advantage over your opponent.' You are expected to do this whether or not your actions might be observed by others.

Like cricket, golf is a slow game in which its 'events' are separated from each other, offering time for reflection and debate. Golf has on the whole managed to maintain its sense of fair play. The writer Stephen Chalke recalls

> half-watching a tournament on television in which the two lead-ing competitors were playing one of the last holes of the final round. One drove his ball into thick rough and had five minutes in which to find it. If he failed, he would suffer a penalty – two shots, I think – which would effectively lose him the tourna-ment. His opponent came across and, in the nick of time, found his ball for him.

* * *

So, to answer the critics of the relevance of 'spirit' in cricket in more detail.

First, vagueness. The maxim 'the Spirit of Cricket' is *meant* to be vague, offering pointers towards attitudes of mind that are to be expected and hoped for from players and others involved in the game.

In the 1970s, Insole, then chair of the committee responsible for top-level cricket, held annual meetings with the county captains. One message he repeated each year was: 'You can drive a coach and horses through the Laws of cricket.' In other words, the Laws don't cover everything; they *can't* cover everything, and it's wrong to imagine there might be a formula or algorithm that would be applicable to all situations. There will always be cases that arouse uncertainty, strange events, shrewd but dubious actions, behaviour motivated by malice or contempt, that the Laws don't specifically address or take into account. And spirit covers more, occupies a wider space, than action.

Atherton himself wrote of the late New Zealand cricketer, Martin Crowe, who sadly died from cancer in 2016:

> Martin viewed his illness, initially, as an opportunity, given that it allowed him to confront the demons and the man that, he felt, cricket had made him into. So, latterly, his instincts for the game and people in it were invariably sound: he was against rampant ego, selfishness, boorishness and bullying (the takeover at ICC by the big three countries made him livid).

This seems to me an excellent expression – and indeed expansion – of what the Spirit of Cricket is getting at. It suggests that Atherton's remark about 'meaningless guff' is not his whole opinion on the matter. 'Sound instincts for the game and people in it' strikes me as more or less equivalent to 'spirit of cricket'.

Certainly, the Spirit of Cricket doesn't, and isn't intended to, offer solutions to most specific controversies: it does not adjudicate on 'walking'. There are arguments on each side. The words in the Preamble don't settle such issues.

But this doesn't mean that they are useless or meaningless. When controversies occur, a good spirit will significantly alter the way the argument is conducted. And Atherton's description of Crowe's later opinions is far from empty.

Indeed, in 2020, Atherton modified his views, writing:

> The spirit of cricket has become one of the game's great strengths and weaknesses. A strength because it reminds everyone that the Laws are found wanting from time to time in a game that has travelled far from its roots, and that fundamental decency and respect lie at the heart of a good contest. It is a weakness because, with that vibrant flowering, the spirit of cricket has come to mean different things to different people.

A different tone from earlier, to be sure. But Atherton still thinks it a weakness that people come to different conclusions in practice. And he still implies that all *could*, in principle, be made clear via the Laws.

Many of the world's most treasured moral precepts have this indeterminate quality. Think of the Golden Rule. The Hindu version is: 'Make right conduct [*dharma*] your main focus; treat others as you treat yourself.' In Islam, we find: 'None of you truly believes until he wishes for his brother what he wishes for himself.' Judaism states: 'You should love your neighbour as yourself.' (And the story is told in the Talmud of a follower asking the sage Hillel to teach him the whole of the Torah while standing on one foot; the reply came: 'That which is hateful to you, do not do to another, this is the whole Torah, and the rest is [*mere*] commentary'.) Christianity asks us to: 'Do unto others as you would have them do unto you.' Finally, Buddhism exhorts: 'Hurt not others with that which pains yourself.' (This motto has to be modified or amplified for sadists and masochists.)

It's true that noble phrases may be used blandly, turned into mere jargon. They may be spouted without thought, as platitudes. This tends to happen when sport takes refuge in management speech, as with the phrase 'Stay with the process', much in vogue in the *The Test: A New Era for Australia's Team*, released in 2020. This series was based on many hours of footage shot in the team's dressing room over several months. The phrase is used to urge players to focus on the next ball, to stay in the present, to avoid dwelling on near-misses or recent strokes of luck. But when it's voiced, some players' faces go blank, rather like students exposed to academics revelling in jargon. There is a risk of an air of deferential dullness rather than a deepening of energy and conviction.

Generalisations need to be balanced by vivid examples, platitudes require life to be breathed into them by narratives, by stories in which individuals doing unique things are memorably depicted. The golden rule was illuminated and particularised by the story of the 'good Samaritan'. Having a range of stories, with sometimes subtle differences, challenges lazy thinking. Noticing the momentary delay in Ashwin's 'Mankading' of Buttler focuses our attention on how apparently small differences create radically different cases, and therefore different conclusions, about the spirit and integrity (or their lack of it) of actions that fall under the same general description.

Great leaders, perhaps particularly religious leaders, combine both forms of leadership; they also combine vivid exemplary stories with unsaturated maxins.

One uncomfortable outcome of such open-endedness is factionalism between followers, all of whom are liable to claim to be the true inheritors. This is how schisms occur, along with accusations of heresy. Freud referred to 'the narcissism of small differences'.

But despite the fact that fundamental precepts may be claimed by vying groups to support their own prejudices and local values, and to scorn those whose culture differs from their own, such maxims have a valuable and universalising aspect. They offer aspirations. They sustain commitments to values such as fair play and honesty. They support our resolve not to descend to cheating.

Such maxims are placeholders for an attitude that is essential for society to run smoothly and with a degree of fairness. Advocating a good spirit is like advocating truth, and being vigorously opposed to 'fake news' and to the idea that one can believe or state or do whatever one chooses. In cricket, it (or cricket's version of it) offers those who play and enjoy the game a vision of a better self and encourages a healthy setting for legitimate rivalry and competition.

The notion of a spirit of cricket advocates respect without resort to mere obedience; implicitly, it warns against what Atherton said Crowe came to reject so forcefully: 'rampant ego, selfishness, boorishness and bullying'. It doesn't and shouldn't tell us what constitutes respect on every given occasion, nor does it attempt to spell out precisely what deserves respect.

Rather than prescribing, or proscribing, *specific* behaviours, the Preamble *orients* players and others. It is a nudge, a reminder. It offers a moral framework, hinting at values that both underlie and go beyond the laws of the game.

Second, critics suggest that the Spirit of Cricket is inevitably used as propaganda for local customs or prejudices. My view is that this is always a risk, but that doesn't mean it's inevitable.

I agree with ex-fast bowler and now commentator, Ian Bishop, that social conditioning is often the predominant factor in what some group or other feels is correct. As we have seen, there are different social or even regional norms.

Here are two instances from Test cricket where there is no absolute answer about what the right outcome should have been, in which tribal loyalties might have made people insist on their rights.

In 1974, at Port-of-Spain, Trinidad, Tony Greig ran out Alvin Kallicharran when the batsman was walking off the field before the umpire had called 'Time'. Greig had rushed back from silly mid-off to pick up the ball as it rolled towards extra cover, turned, saw Kallicharran out of his ground at the bowler's end and threw down the stumps. It was a moment of hyped-up opportunism rather than a cynical act. Rather similarly, Ian Bell was run out when, on the last ball before tea, against India at Trent Bridge in 2011, incorrectly believing the ball had gone for four, he had begun to walk off when the stumps were broken. Both Kallicharran and Bell were later reinstated, though both had correctly been given out according to the letter of the law. In each case, the fielding sides were willing to accede to the reversal of the initial decisions.

Though one might hope for such generosity (or for not wanting to be seen as mean-minded) – generosity shown by England in Trinidad, by India at Trent Bridge – it's not something one should rely on. In each case the reversal of the decision was possible only because immediately ensuing intervals allowed for second thoughts and negotiation.

The problem is not so much the existence of a spirit of cricket as its being used to justify one's own often passionate views, when what's being advocated *is*, as Bishop said, the outcome of merely local conditioning. But disagreements aren't always a matter of our lot occupying the moral high ground and yours being beyond the pale. There will sometimes be honest and honourable differences of opinion and feeling about what's within the spirit and what's not. We may even come to see our own prejudices as the result of the provinciality of our conditioning.

Once again, the point goes far beyond sport. Here are two small examples of cultural variations that are simply a matter of difference;

neither side is right or superior, neither is wrong or inferior. First, if you go from London to New York, you need to remind yourself that New Yorkers don't say 'please' and 'thank you', but this doesn't mean they are bad-mannered. Second, in India people eat with their fingers, whereas in the West we commonly use cutlery. The Indian custom involves washing hands immediately before and after what is a controlled and delicate use of fingers. Gradually, the child becomes less messy, learning not to allow food to get above the first joint of each finger. In the West, the general culture teaches us that to eat a meal with one's fingers is indelicate, crude, though we do resort to using fingers for toast and marmalade. We have to learn to use a knife and fork. There are even cultural differences in how we use cutlery; in some families and cultures it's rude to use the fork as a spoon or shovel. When eating peas, must we always balance them on the back of the fork, or stab them one at a time on the prongs?

These cultural ways seem to me simply to be differences, not gradations in civilisation. But there are people who regard eating with fingers, say, as a matter of inferiority. One England cricketer told me how he was having a meal in an Indian home during a tour. He was extremely attracted to a young woman present; she to him. They were secretly playing footsie under the table. Then the food arrived and she, naturally, ate in the Indian way. He was shocked and instantly put off. He removed his foot. His feeling was that this was a primitive practice. No doubt as a child he, like many in the West, had been told off for, or at least discouraged from, picking up food with his hands.

I think his prejudice meant he missed his chance. Perhaps that was, in the long run, good luck for both parties.

7

WHEN ALL IS SAID AND DONE . . .

'Sledging is infantile playground behaviour, isn't it?'

Tom Cartwright

Racial sledging is rightly regarded as unacceptable, and this view is embodied in ICC's tariff for such abuse on the field (a ban for up to three Test matches, or the equivalent), as opposed to the maximum penalty for non-racist abuse, a one-Test ban.

A cause célèbre occurred in the 2008 Second Test at Sydney between Australia and India. It became known as 'Monkeygate'. Not long before, ICC had announced 'zero tolerance' of racial abuse and had initiated a new requirement to report any alleged occurrence.

With Australia in some trouble on 193 for 6 on the first day, Andrew Symonds, on 30, edged Ishant Sharma to keeper M. S. Dhoni. He was given not out by umpire Steve Bucknor. He finished the day on 130, the innings ending next morning with him 162 not out.

At that time, the Australian Board allowed players to comment in the press during matches. Symonds wrote, provocatively: 'I saved Australia by not walking.'

Feeling had already been running high between the teams. The previous year, Indian crowds at One-Day Internationals had taunted Symonds, who is half indigenous Australian, with monkey-chants in India, and there had been accusations that off-spinner Harbhajan Singh had racially abused him in Mumbai, referring to bananas. The matter was dealt with between the teams, and there were promises that whatever had happened between the players would not be repeated.

Nevertheless, on the third day, when Harbhajan was supporting Sachin Tendulkar in an important stand, he dug out a yorker from fast bowler Brett Lee to fine leg, and, as he completed a single, tapped Lee on the backside with his bat, saying: 'Well bowled, mate.' Symonds piped up: 'You're not our fucking mate,' whereupon Harbhajan was alleged to have said: 'And you're a fucking monkey.' The umpires reported this, and Harbhajan was charged. He had, remember, what lawyers refer to as 'previous', that is, he had (presumably) made similar comments a year before. He had also had belligerent exchanges with other Australian players.

At the hearing, held before match referee Mike Procter, it emerged that at the crucial time the stump microphones had not been working. There was therefore no direct auditory evidence. Symonds himself, Michael Clarke and Matthew Hayden all said they had heard the word 'monkey' used by Harbhajan. Ricky Ponting, Australia's captain, who left the field briefly to file a report (as he was obliged to do), said he himself had heard nothing.

Chetan Chauhan, India's manager, retorted that Ponting had been dismissed by the off-spinner several times, implying that he wanted him off the tour. Chauhan's attitude seemed to be: 'The Aussies are the biggest abusers' – but that is hardly a defence. Murdered murderers, burgled burglars, should not, on account of their own records, forfeit the right of redress. Nor was Chauhan's defence consistent: first he maintained that Harbhajan never said it, second that he spoke no English (partly true – his English would improve only years after his retirement, when he became a commentator). Third, he added, 'We Indians are not racist,' bringing as evidence a book that included pictures of the monkey god (Hanuman) with a human body and a monkey's head. In other words, the accused didn't say it, he couldn't say it (no English), and if he did say it, it was a compliment, not a slur.

Tendulkar, Harbhajan's batting partner, reported that at the moment in question he had heard Symonds going after Harbhajan repeatedly in a verbal assault, but not what Harbhajan replied; he could not have heard an ordinary conversation at that distance (presumably about the length of the pitch, as each batsman had completed the single).

Procter found Harbhajan guilty as accused and banned him for racist abuse for three Tests. There was a great hoo-ha, and speculation that the Indian team would go home in protest.

Many journalists took the Indian side, assuming the worst of the Australians. Peter Roebuck, in the *Sydney Morning Herald*, laid into them (without knowing the facts). Matthew Engel (the *Guardian*) and Mihir Bose (BBC) were more cautious, trying to get more information.

The Indian Board appealed, and the team stayed on. The rules stated that the case now had to be held in front of a judge, and New Zealand High Court Judge John Hansen was appointed to preside. The appeal was delayed until after the last (fourth) Test, in Adelaide, which Harbhajan played in, having not been selected for the third, at Perth.

At this second hearing, the Australian cricketers turned up casually dressed, in thong-sandals, which did not make a good impression. The Indian approach was now different. They admitted that Harbhajan had uttered offensive remarks. Tendulkar now recalled that he had heard Harbhajan abuse Symonds, calling him in Punjabi a 'mother-fucker'; the word that implies this – *ma(n)ki* – could be mistaken for the English word 'monkey'. But, Tendulkar stated, he had not said anything racist. And captain Anil Kumble reported that Harbhajan denied making a racist remark.

(It may be harder for players or umpires who speak only English to be sure of abuse or its precise nature when English is at best a second language for some of those involved. In the Second Test at Brisbane in 1982, Javed Miandad, captaining Pakistan, was accused of swearing at batsmen. His defence was that he wasn't saying 'Fuck off', he was repeatedly calling on his team-mate, Ijaz Faqih, 'Faqih, Faqih, Faqih'. A linguistically sophisticated Indian observer tells me that the latter would usually have been addressed by compatriots as Ijaz, not Faqih. Indeed, the use of English as the official language of international cricket, though inevitable in a game played largely by Commonwealth countries, may feed some resentments in India and elsewhere about assumptions of an old Anglo-Saxon sense of superiority.)

Hansen's verdict was that the accusation of racism was unproven. Criticising both teams for their abrasive behaviour, he cancelled the ban on Harbhajan, finding him guilty of a lesser charge (of using abusive language), for which he was fined half his match fee. Hansen admitted afterwards that he might have imposed a more serious penalty had he been made aware of the bowler's previous (alleged) transgressions.

One man whose career was cut short by this whole event was umpire Bucknor; India refused to have him stand in subsequent matches, and the Sydney Test was his last. But the person apparently most affected was Symonds. He 'went off the rails' and never recovered. He was sent home from the 2009 T20 World Cup, his third exclusion within a year for disciplinary reasons that included excessive alcohol use. His friend Hayden said that he 'couldn't help him'. Ponting, his captain, criticised Cricket Australia's handling of the event, saying that their lack of support for the team, and in particular for Symonds (arising, he said, from their alleged eagerness to do a compromise deal with the BCCI), led to a premature end to the latter's Test career. Symonds retired from all forms of cricket in 2012 at the age of thirty-seven.

* * *

Racist sledging is only one type of sledging, and only one form of racism in sport. Whatever its content, sledging goes against the spirit of cricket. The quote from Tom Cartwright continued: 'The wicketkeeper is expected to orchestrate all this noise, and the players are telling you all the time who they are going to target. It's pathetic.'

The word 'sledging' (in this context) seems to be an Australian usage describing an activity that is by no means confined to Australians but perhaps finds its natural home in that culture (though of course there are many Australians who have no truck with it at all).

I'm aware that there are grey areas in which it is hard to draw a sharp line between boorish threats at one end of the spectrum, and ordinary rough banter and legitimate unsettling at the other. One *could* perhaps use the term to cover any verbal comment directed at the batsman.

But the etymology of the term links its cricketing use with Anglo-Saxon 'slaegen', meaning to strike violently. I think we should restrict it to violent or abusive use of words, ruthless insult – hitting someone with a (usually metaphorical) sledgehammer.

Some abuse is disgusting, beyond the pale. I heard reports of a nasty jibe at Jonny Bairstow, referring to the suicide of his father, David. Such sledging (on and off the field) refers, triumphantly, atrociously, to horrendous losses suffered by the abused. In 2020,

Manchester City supporters mocked Manchester United fans with images of a crashing plane – referring to the Munich disaster of 1958, when twenty-three passengers died, eight of them United players.

Sledging and verbal abuse are obvious targets for disciplinary action, being easier to legislate against and find evidence for than more hidden matters of attitude and basic assumption. But it is not always easy to differentiate sledging (or culpable sledging) from a legitimate unsettling of one's opponents.

＊　＊　＊

Steve Waugh, the tough, thoughtful and shrewd captain of a highly successful Australian team, shifted the moral landscape of cricket in his use of the term 'mental disintegration'. Every team rightly wants to make the opposition do their job less well. But if the aim of mental disintegration is actually achieved, people on all sides are devastated. Remember Jonathan Trott, one of England's best batsmen, who in 2013–14 had his confidence shot to pieces by the fast bowling of Mitchell Johnson, by the sledging of the Australian side, and by his own perfectionist expectations of himself. Physically and mentally shell-shocked, he fell apart. He had to leave the tour, and not long afterwards retired relatively early.

When the great Australian fast bowler, Dennis Lillee, ran in to bowl at Perth, the crowd would chant in time with his strides: 'Kill, kill, kill . . . ', a crescendo mounting to a climax as he released the ball. But if someone is seriously harmed, or even actually dies (think of Phillip Hughes, the batsman who died in 2014 after being hit by a bouncer), everyone is appalled.

Waugh first heard the phrase 'mental disintegration' applied in cricket from his captain, Allan Border, who used it during the Sixth Test in 1989 to describe the impact of delaying a declaration against England beyond when they would have expected. He wanted to rub their noses in it.

Both men were uncompromising captains, masters of the steely look, the comments thrown out of the side of the mouth. Words, gestures, gait, tactics all contributed to the effect.

Unsettling and demoralising the opposition is an acceptable aim of competitive sport. It is in my view fine to play on character weaknesses as well as on technical ones. Indeed, there are legitimate ways of provoking an opponent. One might even convey an insulting message.

In 2019, Steve Smith scored a double century at Old Trafford. Next day, a spectator recommended a ruse that might get to him, suggesting that, early in his innings, England put on an occasional bowler, whom Smith didn't rate, to induce him into over-asserting his ego. Such an apparently inconsequential move might puzzle him: 'What on earth are they up to?'

The fan's suggestion appealed to me. During his innings the day before, I too had noticed that this great batsman had taken slow bowler Jack Leach seriously only after the latter had first dismissed Matthew Wade, and then similarly deceived Smith himself in flight, the batsman being lucky that his skied stroke dropped just out of reach between extra cover and deep cover. The final warning came to Smith when he was outrageously fortunate to be recalled after being caught at slip off the same bowler, the delivery having been discovered through the TV replay to have been a no-ball.

In 2008, M.S. Dhoni, then captain of India, brought on batsman Yuvraj Singh to bowl his very slow and hardly turning left-arm 'filth' (in professional jargon) early in Kevin Pietersen's innings. The move riled Pietersen, who called Yuvraj a 'pie-chucker'. But this particular pie-chucker had twice got him out earlier in the tour, once in a Test match, and still made this great batsman look like a novice.

As a batsman, I remember feeling humiliated when Brian Bolus, captain of Nottinghamshire, put every fielder in attacking positions against me. This ploy contributed to my feeling inept; I felt timid and by the same token tempted to show them how wrong they were by extravagant stroke-play. Both tendencies were capable of undoing me.

Humour humanises, turning potential abuse and undermining into banter. Surrey cricketer, Jimmy Ormond, playing in the first of his two Test matches, at the Oval in 2001, was told by Mark Waugh (twin brother of Steve): 'Mate, what are you doing out here? You're no way good enough to play for England.' Ormond had the nerve and presence of mind to reply: 'At least I'm the best player in my own family.'

New Zealand batsman John Wright recently reminded me of an occasion I'd forgotten, when slow bowler Philippe Edmonds and I discussed the field we should place while standing next to Wright at the crease. We spoke, he recalled, about his dourness, about how we needed no deep fielders for him. Wright was secure enough for it to make no difference to how he played. He continued in his own sweet way. He was simply amused by our attempts to provoke him. Doubtless our conversation, itself partly functioning to amuse ourselves, had no impact at all. Edmonds and I could have saved our breath with Wright, but with a less secure person, it might have led to extravagance or an uptight caution.

If such ploys do disturb you, or make you play differently, then I think you have yourself to blame. My feeling about the imposition of this kind of psychological pressure is: if you don't like the heat, don't go into the kitchen. Philosopher Alain de Botton once reacted to an unfavourable review of his work with the protest that it would damage his livelihood. Too bad, I'd say. Write better, find ways of getting your own back, grin and bear it. Tolerate a more austere life. Resisting provocation is the name of the game.

However, to 'demoralise' someone is one thing, to 'disintegrate' them another. Ruthless, malicious, even cruel abuse of any kind is a menace to the game. Moreover, no one knows for sure what the impact will be. Even within a team teasing may become mean, misjudged and undermining. My telling Bob Willis he looked like a wounded camel went beyond the bounds of ordinary teasing. Nor was it helpful. It might have worked better with, and been less upsetting to, Ian Botham.

Is a character weakness just the same, then, from a tactical point of view, as a technical weakness? Is it something simply to be exploited? On the whole, I'd say yes, though be aware of the dangers!

Border-Waugh may become Border-War.

* * *

As in life in general, racism enters sport in complex ways. Racist sledging is only the tip of the iceberg of racism. And racism towards people of colour is so well-documented as hardly to need evidence.

Middlesex cricketer Richard Stewart played fifty-two first-class matches for the county between 1966 and 1968. Known as 'Wes' – which in cricketing parlance of those years could refer only to the great West Indies fast bowler, Wes Hall, who struck fear into many batsmen – our 'Wes' was a gentle man, who bowled at a gentle medium pace. He had, however, an excellent record, taking in those matches 131 wickets at an average of less than 24.

Stewart had arrived in England from Jamaica in 1955, aged ten. In 2012, after paying taxes for five decades, he applied for a passport. He was told by the Home Office that he had overstayed. After years of obstruction and suspicion, he was informed that he was after all entitled to stay, but needed to pay £1,200 to 'naturalise'. He didn't have the money and was unable to persuade officials that the mistake had been theirs, not his. Eventually, early in 2019, he received a passport, but was still waiting for the compensation promised by the government in order to fund the trip he had longed to make to the Caribbean. One priority was to visit his mother's grave. His son Wesley added: 'His dream was that we would all go to the Caribbean and see where he was from.' He died on 15 June in the same year.

Stewart's treatment resulted from the 'hostile environment' policies introduced by the then Home Secretary Theresa May in 2012. His son described him as a 'pioneer of cricket for the Windrush generation and a gentleman'. Having known Wes from playing a few games with him for Middlesex First and Second XIs, I endorse that opinion. His serious look would be gradually overtaken by a long, slow smile. Apparently, he never thought of Britain as a racist country until he came into contact with the Home Office during these distressing last seven years. 'It was blatant discrimination,' his son says. 'The government made him feel like: "You're black, you shouldn't be here. Full stop."'

Racial stereotyping has long been rife in English sport. For decades black footballers were considered to lack discipline and commitment. This view has changed. In the years 2016–19, a high percentage (51.2 per cent) of the England soccer squads selected by Gareth Southgate was black, compared with 36.9 per cent under Roy Hodgson (2012–16) and 22.7 per cent overall since 1978. More generally in the sport, despite efforts to eradicate it, racism seems to be increasing once again.

There have been similar forms of stereotyping in cricket. During the 1980s, in apparently respectable publications, players whose families came from the Caribbean were alleged to lack the kind of resilience that could be relied on in (white) British players (who, we were to assume, never collapse under pressure). Moreover, 'overseas' cricketers playing for England were not, and could not be, as committed to the team's success as whites. One offensive article, in *Wisden Cricket Monthly*, concentrated on black players such as Phillip DeFreitas and Devon Malcolm, who had spent many of their formative years in England, rather than on the white South Africans, such as Robin Smith and Allan Lamb, who had come over as adults as a route into Test cricket.

Had there been no such assumptions, I myself might never have played for England. Tony Greig's selection of me for my first Test, in 1976 at the age of thirty-four, to play against West Indies, along with thirty-nine-year-old John Edrich and forty-five-year-old Brian Close, was based on his conviction that West Indies would lose heart (even 'grovel') if batsmen hardened by experience resolutely stuck it out against their fast bowlers. This belief, in turn, was based in part on experience – he had watched tough Australian batsmen Ian Chappell and Ian Redpath battle successfully in 1975–6 – but also in part on deep-seated ideas about racial characteristics.

During the 1950s and before, it was for West Indies selectors and administrators a foregone conclusion that the captain of the team should be white, or at least light-skinned. Black people were believed – if 'believed' is not too active a word; perhaps it was more a matter of the assumption being ingrained like mould in a Stilton – to have the virtues of children such as spontaneity, enthusiasm and living in the present, but not the cooler, more grown-up virtues of detachment, judgement and rationality. It took a long campaign, itself both intellectual and passionate, led by C. L. R. James as editor of the *Nation* newspaper in Trinidad, to get the great leader Frank Worrell selected in 1960 as captain of West Indies.

Two personal experiences of racist assumptions come to mind. In the 1970s, a member of the cricket Establishment (I'll call him Charles) murmured to me one day in his languid, upper-class drawl: 'The problem with the modern Jamaican, Michael, is that he thinks himself the equal of you or me.' According to his subtext, I suspect that it wasn't only the 'modern Jamaican' who made this error. I too may have been under a similar delusion. Charles's 'we' was a thinly populated category.

And the second. In 1967 I returned from a year at the University of California to Cambridge to continue my postgraduate work. Through the University Accommodation Service I found a room on a busy street, which I liked but which was likely to be noisy. I hesitated. The advisor whispered to me, conspiratorially: 'Don't hang about.

Those Nigerians will get it if you're not quick.' This remark was even more shocking than the episode with Charles, for she had institutional responsibility to look after all students equally. The spirit of the job, one might say, required her to be both fair and transparent. And I had no doubt that her picking out 'the Nigerians' was racist.

Racism is directed not only against black people, nor is it the prerogative of whites.

The stereotyping of Asians makes use of different prejudices from those applied to blacks. In 1951 Geoffrey Howard was about to travel to India and Pakistan as manager of the MCC team; Stephen Chalke writes:

> He had never been to India, he had never managed a tour, he had no support staff, not even a scorer, yet, with just two journalists for company, he was sent off with seventeen players. What another world it was from modern tours, when the support staff outnumber the players and the journalists outnumber both combined. 'What sort of briefing did you get from the MCC?' I asked him. 'Briefing,' he repeated, looking pensively at the gas fire. 'Briefing?' Eventually he found in his memory something that might come in the broad category of a briefing. 'The Secretary of MCC, Colonel Rait Kerr, was a Sapper; he knew India, he'd served there. He came down to Fenchurch Street to see us off for Tilbury and, as we parted, he said to me, "Well, good luck, old boy, rather you than me. I can't stand educated Indians."

Presumably, uneducated Indians are all right because they don't regard themselves as entitled to be on a similar footing to white Englishmen. I suspect the mentality was: if Indians weren't plainly inferior, they were insolent.

By now we know enough about racism to realise that it is systemic, part of general culture and of institutions, and that much of it is unconscious, though including many conscious beliefs. We all have touches of it, I think. We can't help ourselves. We protect our privileged positions. (And I'm aware of the complexity of this 'we').

To give one example: in opposing hatred towards Muslims (sometimes called 'Islamophobia'), the then Foreign Secretary, Jeremy Hunt, remarked in 2018 that we must be 'whiter than white' on this topic. This apparently innocent comment seems to me to contain a subliminal thought that runs counter to the main conscious intention. Hunt wanted to emphasise that we must be absolutely clear in our opposition to religious, racist and cultural prejudice; but the language used to express his thought carries a hint of the idea that white is better than brown or black. (I'm also reminded of public announcements made by the government minister responsible for decimalisation (in the early 1970s) that 'at least three quarters' of British people were in favour of it.)

Freud noticed that unconscious ideas perseverate, causing repeated slips or errors. During the time leading up to what became known as the 'D'Oliveira affair', in 1968, when the selection (and earlier non-selection) of a 'non-white' South African, who had emigrated to England in 1960 and had been playing for England for the previous two years, became a major political controversy, the MCC and people representing it veered one way and another, perseverating with apparent inconsistencies.

First, early in 1968 they rightly asked the South African Cricket Board a direct hypothetical question: would any players selected by MCC to tour South Africa later that year be acceptable in that country? Clearly, the reason for the question was the fact that Basil D'Oliveira was currently a member of the MCC team in the West Indies, and it was important for players, selectors and others to be clear about this context. In March, however, following the advice of Alec Douglas-Home, then Shadow Foreign Secretary, MCC decided not to press for an answer, hoping, first, that the South African government might soften its general stance, and (possibly) second, that D'Oliveira's form would settle the matter – he had been having an unhappy time on tour, so if he was out of contention for selection, invidious issues could be sidestepped, and the risk of premature cancellation avoided. So this key issue remained uncertain. In David Sheppard's words, 'they chose to stumble from one selection or non-selection to another, and hoped that it would be "all right on the night"'.

In June, D'Oliveira was selected for the First Test against Australia. He took two wickets economically, and made England's highest score in the match (87 not out). For the Second Test, he was the one of the twelve left out from the final eleven half an hour before the start, on the grounds that he was not penetrative enough as a bowler. During the next weeks he lost form – which itself might have had roots in the conflicting pressures he faced; from one direction came demands that he be more overtly political in calling out racism, from the other he was being seduced by the prospect of money to step away from Test cricket in order to ensure that the tour took place. He was not included in the teams for the Third and Fourth Tests. For the final Test, at the Oval, he was eventually selected: as a replacement, for an opening batsman, Roger Prideaux, but only after both Barry Knight and Tom Cartwright had been declared unavailable. Then on the second day, Friday 23 August, under immense pressure, he scored 158 in England's first innings. On Tuesday England won the match with five minutes to spare. Despite this, two days later his name was not in the list of sixteen players announced for the upcoming tour of South Africa. The final incongruity came when, in mid-September, he was brought in for the tour as a replacement for the bowling all-rounder, Cartwright.

These inconsistencies, I suggest, may well have represented con-flictual trends of thought and feeling in the minds of those involved. Most if not all were honest; honourable 'according to their lights', that is, according to the complex light cast on the situation by con-scious and unconscious assumptions. The problem was the lights.

* * *

Another form of unconscious cultural racism appears as 'exceptional-ism'. In one cricket team I played in, I heard the comment: 'If "they" were all like Joe, it would be fine,' Joe being one of the players of colour in the team. The 'they' indicates a conglomerating and stereo-typing of blacks (or not-whites).

In his autobiography *Who Am I, Again?* Lenny Henry remembers an example of exceptionalism as part of the casual and crude racism of the 1970s and '80s:

> In the leadup to the TV programme, *New Faces*, I remember somebody saying to me: 'When I say the word "nig-nog", I don't mean you, Len. You're one of us. I mean them other nig-nogs.' I think I just nodded dumbly. Why would somebody say this? Like I was going to say: 'I don't mean racist arsehole. I just mean them other racist arseholes.'

Henry himself regrets his 'lack of teeth', encouraged by his fear and hatred of physical fights, and underpinned by his mother's fierce advocacy of integration.

Exceptionalism is used to deny ubiquitous, overall disparagement. The American dream, whereby Oprah Winfrey and others who have escaped many aspects of the traps of poverty and racial discrimi-nation are extolled as examples of what is possible in that country, enables many to underplay the cumulative trauma inflicted by racial prejudice, as well as by other economic and social disadvantages.

* * *

One way we express and reveal our hidden racism, or at least our insufficient awareness of its insidiousness, is by saying nothing, by avoiding conflict. I think the main reason I remember so sharply those two episodes of flagrant racism – the one about the 'modern Jamaican', the other to do with accommodation – is the shameful fact that I said nothing to disabuse these two people. In keeping quiet, remaining 'neutral', my own compliance with racism (and my lack of courage) appeared.

I did not say to Charles: 'And what else *should* the modern Jamaican think?' or perhaps simply: 'So? How is this a problem?' I did not say to the accommodation woman: 'Excuse me, but did you say *Nigerians?*' Or: 'I'm sorry to hear you say that. I will be writing a letter to the head of this service.' I availed myself the privilege of standing outside the situation rather than speaking up. I preferred not to disturb my comfortable position, by allowing myself to remain, or appear to remain, allied to my interlocutors' superiority and prejudice. I did not want to rock the boat. I sided with the mob-attitude of the privileged.

* * *

Nor is racist prejudice confined to the British. Indian novelist Arundhati Roy writes in 2020: 'The Indian obsession with fair skin is one of the most sickening things about us.' And in his history of Indian cricket, Ramachandra Guha, writing about caste prejudice, describes how the advent of British rule allowed an escape from the pernicious labelling of 'Untouchability' – a set of practices and orientations that ostracised the lowest castes and, even more, those who were outside the caste system ('outcasts'). Many of these people 'flocked to the cantonments and factories set up by the British after their defeat of the Peshwas in 1818.'

Discrimination according to caste has a long history in Hinduism. Rooted in religious beliefs about rebirth and karma, though outlawed in India since independence, it is still a pervasive blight, the sinister underpinning of social status and oppression.

Palwankar Baloo was born in 1875 into the low and despised caste of 'Chamaars', people who worked with leather, killing (sacred) cows for their skins and meat. Working for the army in Poona, Baloo encountered cricket. His first job there had been sweeping and rolling the pitch for the Parsee Club, but soon he bowled at the members, as he also did later at the British Club, learning the art of left-arm spin by copying one Captain Barton, who had a smooth action. He became the star bowler of the Hindus in Poona and subsequently in Bombay, with the sobriquet 'the Wilfred Rhodes of India', after the celebrated Yorkshire and England bowler of that name. His brothers too were talented cricketers.

But their careers and opportunities were studded with controversy in his community. Some higher-caste Hindus were happy to break bread with Baloo, as well as play with him, while others were appalled at the idea. From 1895, Guha writes:

> When Baloo first began playing competitive cricket, the Palwankar brothers had struggled to be included in mixed teams, struggled to be served tea and cakes in the cups and plates used by their fellows, struggled to be rewarded with the leadership status their achievements had called for.

There are echoes here of pre-apartheid South Africa, when sportsmen of colour received trophies at the back doors of pavilions.

The 1920 Quadrangular was the Hindu team's 'most substantial victory to date'. Baloo had been appointed vice captain, leading the team on the field for the last day of the big match against the Parsees after two of his brothers, who had previously withdrawn on the grounds of caste discrimination, were reinstated. In 1922, brother Vithal was elected captain. In his four seasons in this role, the Hindus won the Quadrangular three times.

Guha gives the following verdict on Baloo. He was 'arguably the first great cricketer produced by India, and also a hero and role model among the low castes'.

One feature of the great West Indian teams from the mid-1970s to the mid-1990s was their proper pride, which communicated itself to their compatriots at home and abroad. In post-slavery West Indies, cricket had offered an opportunity (despite resistance and prejudice) for black men to compete on more or less equal terms with white and light-skinned players. In the early 1900s, the success of the likes of fast bowler Archie Cumberbatch and batsman Lebrun Constantine (Learie's father) was a source of deep pride. Later, the (eventual) appointment of a black man, Worrell, as captain enabled the man and woman in the Caribbean street to walk tall, as did the domination of cricket by West Indies under Clive Lloyd and Viv Richards in their years of triumph.

Given the appalling history of slavery and colonialism, it was remarkable that Caribbean cricketers were able to find such pride without undue arrogance or triumphalism; but it would be naive, I think, to believe that there was no trace of retaliation. For the team of 1976, for example, Greig's remark about grovelling was a stimulus to their motivation, intensifying an already passionate determination to make England the ones to do any grovelling. The film *Fire in Babylon*, made in 2010, describes the shaking off of an image of the 'calypso cricketer' who entertained but didn't win, and the firming up of a sense of solid and determined ambition; a transformation, perhaps, from individual flair to absolute commitment to the success of the group.

In the 2020 upsurge of awareness of racism during the 'Black Lives Matter' campaign following the killing of George Floyd by police in Minneapolis, there has been unease, including among some people of colour, at the triumphalist elation shown by protesters who dragged down statues of the slave-owner Edward Colston in Bristol.

I think the scenes were disturbing for contradictory reasons. On the one hand the elation evoked one's own usually secret wishes to 'get our own back', by humiliating and even killing exploiters, bullies, and those who use their power cruelly. We are reminded of our own suppressed or hidden barbarity in reaction to such experiences, actual and imagined. On the other hand, I and others feel uncomfortable also because it has taken episodes like this to hit home with us just how offensive the presence of public statues and honorific street names is and has been for many people. I had a similar jolt when a black professor on TV asked us British whites how we might feel if our public squares and streets had plinths topped by sculptures of Hitler and other prominent Nazis.

*　*　*

I remember conversations I had with Roland Butcher, a fine cricketer born in Barbados and left there with his grandparents at the age of eight when his parents came to England searching for a better life for their children and themselves. He was finally sent for when he was twelve. Butcher was a brilliant stroke-player and fielder. But when he first made his way into the Middlesex side, interspersed with striking successes were too many low scores. I wanted to make him more resolute in his defensive play, particularly early in his innings. In our many long conversations on trips to away matches I encouraged him to be more robust, even aggressive, in defending himself, not only against opposition bowlers, but also in the dressing room and beyond, against both undisguised and implicit racism, as also in response to regular kinds of banter, to which he was sometimes as I saw it over-sensitive – though I'm aware of the risk of setting myself up as arbiter of objectivity in such matters.

I remember using the word 'limp' with regard to some of his defensive shots. I contrasted the aggression and absolute determination that drove on that master of defensive technique, Geoffrey Boycott. I even

117

suggested there was a particular Bajan tendency that prioritised a relaxed and elegant style over total commitment and survival. I asked him to consider the possibility that his limpness represented in him a doubt about his own value. I remember too going through with him one by one the whole Middlesex side at that time (we were in the middle of a successful period), pointing out how each in his own way had a measure of aggression. John Emburey would go red trying to restrain himself when yet another plumb lbw appeal was turned down. Clive Radley, not overtly aggressive, was extremely determined; watching him take a catch in the slips, we could sense the ferocity of his concentration followed by a moment of intense exultation.

When teased in the dressing room, Roland began to stand up for himself more, giving as good as he got. He became more robust, off and on the field. Alongside this development in self-assertiveness, he became a perceptive contributor to group processes within the team – one example being his noticing and pointing out a collective transition from confidence to complacency. He was, too, able to remind us all of how, as soon as a player was left out of the team or side-lined in less obvious ways, teammates were more constrained and awkward in talking to him.

My response to Butcher was, thus, to challenge him as well as to empathise. I asked him to struggle with what had, I thought, become for him second nature. He took on my challenge; recognising his tendency. He worked to change. He became both a better cricketer and a happier, more confident person. I think our conversations were factors in this development.

People who have been downtrodden in their families or their culture cannot undo the past: their most realistic option is to change themselves, refusing to nurse grievances, but also refusing to lie down or go limp when faced with further examples of actual or imagined prejudice. Like a patient in analysis who, urged to give up using her (neglectful) parents as a ball and chain, fought to free herself from this aggrieved constraint, Butcher took up the cudgels (including the bat) on his own behalf, becoming in the process not only tougher and more determined, but also more sympathetic and alert to the plight and reactions of others.

* * *

There is no denying the damage that being the recipient of persistent racism does to people. It is a cumulative trauma. As psychoanalyst Fakhry Davids writes:

> To be black in a white world is an agony. This is because the white world is racist – if you are black, you are seldom allowed to be an ordinary, regular human being. Instead, at every turn you are confronted by hidden stereotypes that can spring to life in a flash, push violently into you, destabilize you and make you think, feel and act in ways that are wholly determined from the outside, as if you yourself had no say in the matter. This can turn even the most innocuous of situations utterly fraught.

Victims victimise themselves. They have a racist persecutor within. This is a corrosive orientation. The person has imbibed the hostile attitude of their environment. I like the phrase 'double consciousness', coined by W. E. B. Du Bois. Like others who are subordinated in oppressive societies, many BAME (black Asian and minority ethnic) children not only have their own take on the world, but find in themselves a second consciousness, a lens transmitted from racist white society through which they view themselves with contempt. I think Butcher had a trace of this, but emancipated himself from it.

Another potential reaction is to switch to being a persecutor of others. Sadism may become an outcome, even an expression, of trauma. The victim becomes the agent, making others, children per-haps, or other vulnerable people, the recipients of their own earlier suffering. Or they turn the tables on people who stand in for their former tormentors, giving them a taste of their own medicine. The form of the relationship has been taken in but is now being expressed in reverse. Its benign version is proper pride.

* * *

But are racial prejudice and oppression worse than other forms of oppression and trauma? Should cricket penalise racial sledging more harshly than other forms of sledging?

As ICC referee in the Monkeygate episode, Procter, who had been brought up in, and lived through, decades of life in apartheid-ruled South Africa, took a stand against racism. (As a result he experienced a backlash from the Indian side for his decision, including being cold-shouldered by an Indian player he had regarded as a friend.)

Procter also felt that Symonds was not an innocent bystander. And this raised for him and for us all the question: is racist abuse necessarily worse than other forms of abuse? If so, why? What about sexist or sexual-orientation abuse, or caste prejudice, or religious persecution, or child abuse? Malicious bullying and discrimination occur also on the basis of class, accent, language or nationality. Mothers, sisters and partners are insulted.

As John Inverarity has said: 'It is understood that racial abuse and sexual-preference abuse are not permitted; then why on earth are other forms of abuse permitted?'

Perhaps one reason for racism being viewed as worse than other abuse is that, in common with gender, we cannot change our physical racial characteristics (though in both cases people now try, often at great expense and disruption to themselves). Also, there is now widespread recognition that the cruelty enacted on the basis of racism has an appalling history, and has certainly not been eradicated. Davids is right: to be black in a white world is (or can be) 'an agony'.

Racism is also absurd. Character has more do with upbringing and cultural influences than with genetics. There is no evidence of genetic racial differences emerging as characterological ones. Generalisations based on colour or race are, I suspect, the most dubious of all. Racial differences are indeed only skin deep.

* * *

We might follow David Sheppard's suggestion in his book title *Bias to the Poor*. Is this a solution? Does such bias correct a more fundamental bias? Will reverse discrimination, for example, turn things around?

In South Africa, the policy of racial quotas or targets for top-level teams, particularly in cricket and rugby, intended to redress racial bias and to address the possibility of underdeveloped potential, has led to court cases and protest. The policy was one reason for Kevin Pietersen's departure to seek qualification in England. The Springboks' first black rugby captain, Siya Kolisi, has said that he did not believe Mandela would have backed quotas for national teams, and argued that racial imbalances could be rectified only through grass-root development. In India, too, job-market and educational reverse discrimination in favour of low-caste Hindus feels, to disadvantaged people from higher castes, unfair and unjust. In many individual cases such policies *are* unfair, even if they may, overall, offer the best possible socio-political solution.

And political correctness may run riot. A friend recounts a story set in the context of a cricket tour in Devon. In the pub after one game, a regular who'd had a few drinks commented to a Barbadian from the visiting team: 'I bet you're a fast bowler.' The captain, a man with a job in social care, had the local thrown out for making a racist remark. Such po-faced righteousness rules out much friendly humour. As Davids said, the most innocuous situations become fraught.

Being too biased in favour of the underprivileged may result in patronising, lifeless correctness.

And when it comes to the law, bias needs, surely, to be in favour of the accused. The onus of proof rests with the prosecution. Evidence for guilt has to be solid.

It is true that we have to accept that being part of the privileged group, which in the so-called West means (on the whole), in racial or ethnic terms, being in the (whitish) majority, is likely to leave us with collectively held assumptions that these privileges are somehow appropriate, even deserved. We tend to prefer the comfort of a group unanimity that often amounts to collective stupidity. We echo each other's biases and blindness. We may fail to notice, let alone empathise with, the experience of people of colour, who have long been recipients of messages like, 'Go back to where you came from.' The excluded, ignored or derided are inevitably more sensitised to such attitudes and actions than those who feel themselves to be (and to varying degrees are) 'haves' rather than 'have-nots'. Both privation and privilege are often invisible to the privileged.

No one can guarantee his or her own neutrality in this area. No one has an infallible claim on objectivity when it comes to questions about sensitivity or over-sensitivity to abuse. Were Sri Lankans unduly sensitive to decisions made by Australian umpires that their hero, Muttiah Muralitharan, sometimes threw the ball? There were, in my view, legitimate grounds for questioning his action. There was also, on the other side, the evidence of his unusual physiology, that made it possible for him to bowl, not throw, a doosra. So, did cultural, even racist, animus enter into the umpires' decisions?

When I spoke bluntly and frankly to Butcher, I risked speaking from a position of superiority, both as captain and white. On the other hand, not to have spoken along the lines I did might also have been patronising – this would have been to treat him as if he would be unable to take on board my comments and think about them;

it might have been arrogant of me to assume that he would inevitably feel belittled by me.

I believe that today *not* speaking out against racism is an ethical defect, resulting often from a failure of imagination as well as of courage. There is no longer space for neutrality in this regard. We become compliant with racism – that is, racist – if we don't actively speak or act against it. It perhaps goes without saying that we must question our own biases. And there is less excuse than before for being blind to the impact of racism, as indeed of other forms of cumulative prejudice of many kinds.

I remember a rich man, who had been to a great English boarding school, drove a Bentley, and was highly cultured. He told me once that the English novel lost its way in the mid-nineteenth century when poverty became a central topic or theme. No doubt he was thinking of writers like Elizabeth Gaskell and Charles Dickens. 'Poverty,' he asserted, 'is merely a damned nuisance.' This is just such a failure of imagination. He spoke of poverty as one who had never experienced it with its systemic impact. Nor had he taken the trouble to try to enter into it through his imagination. It is a 'nuisance' not to have ready cash for your flutter on the horses; or to have to wait for your inheritance. To be born into poverty, to be brought up in the workhouse like Oliver Twist, is utterly different. It becomes part of the warp and weft of a life. This failure of imagination was also a moral failing.

8

RENDER UNTO CAESAR

'He is not to be hanged because he would not stay to
be burned.'

Edmund Plowden (sixteenth-century lawyer)

How do spirit and law inter-relate? And does cricket have an equivalent
to the 'common law', derived from precedent and previous judgment
rather than passed as bills and written down to be consulted, as in
Statute Law?

Implicitly, I think cricket does have elements akin to common
law. When M. J. K. Smith was given out run-out in Johannesburg the
issue was: was the ball 'dead'? That is, had the activity constituting
that delivery been completed? Unlike Appeal Court judges, umpires
are called upon to make almost instantaneous decisions on the field
of play. But in effect what was relevant to this decision, and indeed
to later reflections, was a whole range of cases of what generally and
traditionally has been regarded as constituting a 'dead ball'.

I'm confident that the eventual outcome was correct. It was right
that the decision was reversed. The fact that the keeper caught
and passed the ball to the fielder in one movement, rather than
holding on to it for a few seconds, makes no significant difference.
Wicketkeepers often pass the ball to the slips or short leg in just such
a way, leaving no doubt that this signals closure, 'deadness'. There

was no consideration in this wicketkeeper's action that the ball might be 'alive', that further use might be put to it. The umpire might indeed appropriately have made use of a counter-factual argument: if the 'keeper had carelessly thrown it over the fielder's head, this would not have entitled the batsmen to take a run.

Consulting in this sort of way the meaning and purpose of the law is thus part of practising the law, and this involves a consideration and comparison of cases. The whole process, in the umpire's mind, is subliminal, almost instinctive in its phenomenology. I am inclined to say that this kind of thinking is itself an element in the spirit of the game, in its reliance on a broad agreement, developed over time, on what constitutes a dead or live ball. This kind of agreement exists, though the wording of any rule or law, combined with the particularities of each case, is bound to leave room for occasional contention, especially when disagreement erupts on the spur of the moment on the basis of self-interest.

* * *

From time to time, sporting bodies offer guidelines to their constituency, including to the law enforcers (primarily, umpires and referees). So do governments.

On 23 March 2020, the British government announced its latest strategy for fighting coronavirus. The population were told to stay at home. The only exceptions were: going out for treatment, buying food or medicines (as infrequently as possible), exercising (once a day), and travelling for essential work that could not be done from home. When out, social distancing had to be practised stringently.

There were soon controversies about how these instructions were to be interpreted, including about the standing or status of the rules themselves. Were these definitive rules, intended to be obeyed to the letter, like red traffic lights? Or did they allow room for sensible individual judgement about the criteria for what is and what is not 'essential'? For example, should 'exercise' properly include driving the dog twenty miles to an area of beauty like the Peak District? Should 'going out for treatment' permit driving from London to Durham and back to ensure extended family help in case a four-year-old child becomes ill, when one of the parents has symptoms compatible with having the virus?

One view was that the government ought to have taken responsibility out of the hands of the public, that the rules should be as explicit as possible, without undefined words such as 'essential'. According to this view, there should be as little flexibility as possible: leaving space for discretion would provoke confusion and foment resentment. One person's conception of civic responsibility would for another be an unreasonable expectation: 'why should I give up my job in the interests of general safety while my neighbour selfishly keeps going to work and getting his money?' Having 'guidelines' rather than strict rules ran the risk of creating a more general sense of unfairness that could lead to a damaging mistrust in a government that might be seen to permit 'one rule for us and another for them'. So much was at stake, this line of argument continued, that constant debate and questioning became a dangerous luxury. We should be on a war-footing against the deadly virus. We should build a culture of sacrifice for the common good; this was how the Soviet Union combated superior German forces and armaments in their heroic struggle in the Second World War.

Others disagreed. They emphasised the *principle* behind the new rules, the *grounds* for them – namely, to limit possibilities of infection. If you follow this line, taking your dog for a walk in the hills was within the spirit of the rules, even if it was not, or not strictly, 'essential'. Walking to your allotment, and working or relaxing there in the fresh air with plenty of personal space, should not count as a contravention of the rule to 'stay at home'. In a mature democracy, responsibility is personal not governmental. People should not be infantilised, nor should they be deprived of their liberty. They should be encouraged to make their own judgements. We ought to give weight to the spirit and purpose of the guidelines.

My own view was, and is, that the British government, with its agenda of supporting, with indeed its eagerness to trumpet, traditional freedoms, was unwilling to be as tough as some countries such as New Zealand and Australia, not to mention South Korea and Germany. They sent mixed messages, communicating a lack of rigour in thinking. This led, among populace and police, to unnecessary levels of uncertainty.

My general inclination is to assign and take on personal responsibility where possible. Nevertheless, in this case I believe that the gravity of the threat required the more stringent approach. No form of words can cover every conceivable case of ambiguity and potential disagreement, but I would have liked the government to have been as clear as they possibly could be that these were not 'mere' guidelines or recommendations. The government tried to get the best of both worlds, when they should have opted for a firmer stance.

* * *

The distinction between letter and spirit applies to law itself. The law can be 'an ass'. Justice is a more complex notion than mere legality. Obsessive over-regard for wording may leave out too much. As with other activities there is more to law than the rules that constitute it. It's also the case that well-thought-out drafting is a vital element in the achievement of justice and fairness.

The 'rule of law' has been given 'thin' and 'thick' definitions. A thin one, prioritising factors like transparency and clarity, regards the absence of human rights as no impediment to this title. Tom Bingham, Lord Chief Justice of England from 2001 to 2009, roundly rejected this in favour of a 'thick' definition, one whose scope embraces human rights. Having transparent and well-organised laws is not enough. The apartheid regime offered detailed and transparent rules; but we would rightly refuse to accept its legal system as amounting to a 'rule of law'.

Threats to security frequently provoke demands to strengthen the forces of law and order; this practice often weakens the rule of law. Thus, in Northern Ireland during 'the Troubles', the British authorities hooded and abused suspects. Later, the USA set up its internment camp at Guantánamo Bay, specifically to be a place beyond the reach of the normal protections offered by law. Military tribunals were instituted with lower requirements of proof; *habeas corpus* could be evaded; and torture (waterboarding and other inhumane procedures) was instituted and regularised. These procedures were 'justified' in the interests of security.

We need to respect both the letter of the law and its spirit. As Jesus said when people were outraged by the apparent laxity in some of his invective against obsessive religious legalism: 'Render unto Caesar that which is Caesar's, render unto God that which is God's.'

We are inclined to wish that matters of spirit, expressed in behaviour and especially in attitude, might be definable; made, as in the detail of the law, more specific. One reason is that we are happier with precision, which removes much ambiguity; another is that we are inclined to view the material and measurable as more real than the often un-measurable emotional/mental.

I think this tendency has grown. In 2019, a sports psychologist who worked for a Premier League football club was told: 'If you use the word "spirit" here today, you'll be picking up your unemployment form tomorrow.' The 'science' of sport has had a good run for its money. Today, we need to be reminded of the spirit of sport, and to recognise the importance within it of the inner attitudes involved. Rather than regarding scientific, technical and legally worded data and advice as the last word, we need to access a broader understanding.

The Preamble to the Laws of cricket (about spirit) and the Laws themselves have very different purposes. Yet it is important to realise that ethical and spirit issues are often expressed in laws or rules. We need a moral sense, both for good law, and to appreciate and maintain the social framework for activities governed by law.

For instance, law comes into play in order to protect citizens (and others) from arbitrary assault. Indeed, Magna Carta pronounced in 1215: 'No free man shall be seized or imprisoned, or be dis-seized of his freehold, liberties or free customs: or be outlawed or exiled; or in any other wise destroyed; nor will we proceed with force against him, nor condemn him, except by lawful judgement of his peers, or by the law of the land.'

Julian Elliott Photography/Getty Images

The emblem of the Central Criminal Court, the Old Bailey, is a pair of scales, a matter of weighing the evidence on each side of a case. The figure of Lady Justice, which holds the scales, is blindfolded – presumably implying not that justice is blind, but to represent the idea that it does not look favourably towards any person, group or class.

Lawmakers too have to balance different interest groups and considerations – employers and employees, children and parents, privacy
and surveillance. One might say that the spirit of the law of the land is
to be found in the purposes of the law – is it just and fair to all, does it
intrude into people's lives no more than necessary, is it proportionate
to the inconvenience or safety of the individual and the population
at large? Law-making in any field may be used to enforce power and
oppression, but when this is so, these motives are disguised; changes
of law are at least dressed up as conducive to greater safety or balance.

The laws or rules of a game have similar purposes. The laws of
cricket, and the playing conditions for particular competitions, are
constantly being reviewed and sometimes revised with this sort of
intention. Balance is necessary between batsmen and bowlers,
between different types of bowlers, between attack and defence.
In cricket, changes to the lbw law, for example, have had as their *raison
d'être* a sense of fairness that weighs up the respective advantages to
batsman and bowler, to batting and fielding sides.

Safety considerations have been another important criterion for
modifications to laws or to regulations for particular contexts. Until
the 1970s, first-class cricket was often played on uncovered pitches.
In England at least, these would often help the spin bowler after rain.
The run-ups, footholds and follow-through areas were then often too
wet for faster bowlers to be able to bowl at full pace. However, when
covering extended to these areas, fast bowlers too had solid under-
foot conditions. The result was that on some drying pitches the ball
would rear dangerously from a good length. When this happened
at speed, conditions made batting virtually impossible, even lethal.
The consequence was that uncovered pitches became a thing of
the past at all levels of the game where covering was regularly and
efficiently available. This was not a change to the laws, but to the
playing conditions for Test and county cricket. One main reason for
it was safety, another was balance.

At times, however, recognition of risks to batsmen has led to over-reaction. At one stage in my career, the occasional injury produced by bouncers led to severe restrictions on their use. Lower-order batsmen were for a while protected by umpires from facing even the occasional bouncer, sometimes when they had come in as night-watchmen or had stayed at the crease for a long time. Protection of this kind seemed to me like hobbling fast bowlers. It was as if the great sprinter Usain Bolt were to have his legs tied together when racing against inferior runners. This regulation, or instruction to umpires, went against the balance of the game.

But however careful and well-drafted the laws and regulations are, law cannot cover everything. The playing of games relies on unwritten conventions, shared values and a spirit of cooperation and collegiality.

* * *

When I began to think about the spirit of cricket and its relation to its Laws, I found myself remembering the famous judge, Lord Denning. I recall him in the 1970s as an avuncular figure with a Hampshire burr and a reputation for prioritising justice over narrow legality. I had a sense that his approach was to make common sense central to the framing and interpretation of law. There was much good in this, but many lawyers were concerned that, under the guise of a broader objectivity, he smuggled in personal prejudices to some of his judgments and reviews. Peter Leaver, QC, remembers conversations about the merits of an appeal: 'If we get Denning we have a good chance, but if not, the chances are slim.' This was, he commented, no way to run the law.

Leaver told me that it is not only in Statute Law that lawyers are permitted to make use of other factors as well as the final statute – for example, of earlier drafts, committee minutes and White Papers. In cases involving commercial contracts, courts regard as of prime importance that their judgments smooth the wheels of commerce. Common law too (the body of law constituted by past judicial decisions, whereby disputes are, rightly, settled according to precedent) is 'in modern times' permitted and accustomed to adopt a 'purposive construction' or 'interpretation' of law. This means that it is now considered important to get to the purposes that made the precedents relevant.

Valuing the acquisition of such additional information on the grounds that it may give accurate information about the intentions of the lawmakers marks a radical opposition to what Leaver referred to as 'black letter' law, that is, interpretation of the law that restricts itself to the wording of the written statute or past judgment.

One locus of divergence occurs in the US Supreme Court, where the crucial divide is not only that between conservatives and liberals, but also between those who think the Constitution should be interpreted according to the letter of the original law and those who interpret it in the light of current conditions.

In fact, notwithstanding the recent trend, associated with Denning, this 'modern' approach to the law has a long history, and the distinction has been controversial for centuries.

Taking the purposes of law into account involves getting to what is essential in the law. It also involves avoiding absurd consequences if the law is taken literally.

During the reign of Edward II (1307–1327) it was a felony for a prisoner to break out of prison. But this statute did not extend to a prisoner breaking out when the prison was on fire. As sixteenth-century lawyer Edmund Plowden succinctly put it: 'He is not to be hanged because he would not stay to be burned.'

Judge Nigel Peters, QC, remembers acting in the more recent case of *McMonagle v Westminster City Council* (1989), which was decided by the Appellate division of the House of Lords, the forerunner of today's Supreme Court. McMonagle was prosecuted for running a sex-encounter establishment – a 'peep show' – without a licence.

The legislation stated that a licence could be granted only for activities that were 'not unlawful'. It was argued on the company's behalf that they could not be convicted of trading without a licence as the operation involved unlawful activities and therefore did not fall under the law as written. This argument was not accepted in the lower court. McMonagle was given leave to appeal to the House of Lords, where, treating the words 'not unlawful' as surplus to requirements, the House struck them out. Lord Bridge said of his own judgment that it imputed an unusual degree of ineptitude to the draughtsman, but 'the presumption that every word in a statute must be given some effective meaning is a strong one, but the Courts have on occasion been driven to disregard certain words or phrases when, by giving effect to them, the operation of the statute would be rendered insensible, absurd or ineffective to achieve its evident purpose.'

It could not, that is, be regarded as a sensible intention of the law-makers that the requirement for a licence should be cancelled on the grounds that its activities were illegal. To interpret it in this literal way would indeed be to make an ass of the law.

So, on the one hand, purposive interpretation of the law may bring law closer to justice and fairness. On the other hand, leaving room for the intentions of the lawmakers risks allowing too much room for the prejudices and biases of the judges themselves – as was alleged by critics of Denning. Intentions are, on the whole, less easily established and more subjectively interpreted than matters of material fact and literal meaning.

The law is, and has to be, more specific and detailed, less aspirational and vague, than spirit. There is, however, a close connection between them. The law encompasses issues of spirit, purpose and a sense of fair play. Acknowledging the purpose requires consideration of broader questions of fairness and balance.

* * *

One arena in which the controversy over 'spirit' vs 'letter' comes sharply into focus is religion. When Jesus was provocatively challenged by orthodox and legalistic religious leaders asking him to throw the first stone at a woman taken in adultery, he took a stick and drew or wrote something in the dust. Possibly he was, as Rowan Williams suggests in *Writing in the Dust*, playing for time, giving himself the chance to think. Jesus's answer was brilliant: he neither condoned adultery nor supported the cruel punishment. He simply said: 'Let him who is without sin cast the first stone.'

I first came across Williams's ideas through this little book, in which he reflected on the terrible events of 9/11. On that day, he happened to be making a recording in a studio a few blocks from the World Trade Center, where he was trapped for several hours, and had to be escorted to safety through the dust-filled streets. He argues for the need to move beyond the inevitable fear, anger and wish for revenge evoked by that appalling attack (and others like it). Without denying these powerful emotions, can we refrain from *generalising* our condemnation to a whole group? Moving beyond simple condemnation towards an effort to understand where such terrorism and murderousness might come from is a move from a superficial moral stance to a deeper response of the spirit.

Jesus persistently went beyond what was laid down in religious law at the time. He regularly warned of the risk of losing empathy as a result of narrow dedication to the law. Righteousness easily segues into being a cover for hypocrisy. He emphasised human fallibility. In the case mentioned above, he in effect asked the executioners to reflect on their own dishonesty and unfaithfulness before acting.

Indeed, one of his themes, one of the reasons why religious zealots sought his death, was his questioning of unthinking or merely ritualistic applications of the law. When criticised for allowing his followers to pick grain on the Sabbath, he responded: 'The Sabbath is made for man, not man for the Sabbath.'

He was not, though, impugning or disregarding the law. In fact he said that he came 'not to abolish Law but to fulfil it' – that is, to fill it out, to make it more human, more closely related to lived virtue than to a surface observance of rules and rituals.

Legality focuses most on the *external* application of the law. Primitive morality is content to remain at the level of an eye for an eye, of immediate gut reaction, and of laws that allow savage punishments across the board. An enlarged spiritual/moral attitude goes beyond these considerations, calling for a more self-reflective, more nuanced, more inner response. Jesus again: 'Thou shalt not commit adultery. But . . . whoever looketh on a woman to lust after her hath committed adultery with her already in his heart'.

Some of Freud's objections to religion are based on its elements of obsessional neurosis. But this is only one element in religious belief and practice. Moreover, ritual may be not so much an end in itself as a reliable opportunity for reflection, and a symbol for a deeper truth. Outer forms of ritual and observance may represent, and even lead to, grace and inner change. Sacraments have been defined (by Augustine) as 'an outward and visible sign of an inward and invisible grace'.

All religions face similar conflicts, similar arguments over the role of ritual and sacrament, similar splits between fundamentalism and spirituality, between faith and works, intentions and deeds.

And no religion, no serious enterprise, however high-minded, is exempt from the tendencies either to over-rate external practices at the expense of deeper values, or to undervalue such rules and practices. Both these risks apply to us psychoanalysts. We may either make a shibboleth of five times weekly work, or undervalue the importance of intensity, regularity and open-endedness in helping to deepen the process. During the Covid-19 crisis, in moving to online sessions with patients we have been forced to be more flexible in ideas about what is acceptable technique. We find that not only is online work better than nothing; in some cases, and in some ways, the process can be deepened as a result of this enforced change of setting.

(I like the scurrilous (and fictitious) story about the analyst discovered by a colleague to have been sleeping with his patient. 'It's all right', the colleague says, 'provided he did it five times a week.')

*   *   *

As in law and religion, the rules of a game overlap with its spirit. When as Middlesex captain I wished to forfeit our innings (in a heavily rain-affected match against Surrey in 1977), the umpires were doubtful whether this was permitted in the Laws. I left the field when Surrey had lost 8 wickets in their first innings to ask this question of Donald Carr, the secretary to the Test and Cricket Board. He could see the point of my request, but concluded that it was not allowed in the Laws or Playing Conditions. We were therefore required to face one ball of our first innings before declaring, and thus to waste ten or eleven minutes. By the following season, however, the law had been changed to allow forfeiture. The lawmakers thus quickly perceived a 'mischief' or 'absurdity' in the Laws, and, as soon as they could, changed them. It was as if the Appeal Court had recognised that no purpose was served in prohibiting a bold, positive move. Cricket's lawmakers extended the notion of 'declaring an innings closed' (which amounts to forfeiting whatever remains of an innings), to include 'forfeiting the entire upcoming innings'.

This decision, though of minimal significance, has some structural similarity to the Supreme Court's decision in 2019 that the proroguing of Parliament for five weeks was wrong. The mischief undone by the Supreme Court in that case was the government's attempt to limit unnecessarily the time available for Parliament to challenge its policy on Brexit. The government had given no sound reason why the gap should be five weeks, and not, say, two. And the court wished to prevent the underlying threats posed by misuse of prorogation that of demolishing a fundamental feature of democracy.

Indeed, many discussions about possible changes in laws or playing conditions for cricket revolve around questions of purpose. When the reverse sweep became used more frequently in limited-overs cricket, and even on occasion in the longer forms of the game, further variations developed, such as swivelling or jumping so that as the ball was being bowled the batsman changed from a right-handed to a left-handed stance (or vice versa), or as when hands on the bat were changed so that the bottom hand became the top hand. All these variations led to discussions among lawmakers and advisors, as well as between cricket people in general, about the likely consequences. Was there potential mischief in this innovation? Or did the increased flair and range permitted, along with the risks involved, make the game more lively and fascinating? Were all forms of the stroke unfair on bowlers, who have to declare which hand they are going to bowl with in advance? Or were only some forms unfair?

Further questions were raised about the application of lbw laws when this switch from being a right-hander to being a left-hander occurred, especially if there was the jump from one to the other. A batsman is not liable to be lbw if the ball pitches outside his leg stump: should he be deemed to have two leg stumps if he makes this sudden switch? Or two off stumps? One problem in any further complication in law along these lines was the potential for confusion among umpires, who would have to decide in a flash whether the particular form of reverse sweep made a change in what was to be called the 'leg' or 'off' stump. (The outcome, which I agreed with, was that the new stroke, exciting as it is, would always carry an element of risk for the batsman, so there was no need to further complicate the laws on lbw.)

The laws may be modified as a result of new thinking about its purposes and the mischiefs of traditional attitudes. Such a shift occurred in the 2017 version of the Laws with regard to 'Mankading'. As we saw, the act of running out the non-striker for backing up too soon was for many years deemed to be unsporting, though it was not against any cricket law. If the bowler took this action, umpires tended to ask the captain of the fielding side if he wished to withdraw the appeal. The umpire was in effect saying: the purpose of the law was not to get a wicket by this kind of trickery; are you sure you wish to be responsible for such an act? Or would you prefer to withdraw the appeal?

Now the emphasis has changed, taking account of other purposes, in particular that the non-striking batsman is acting illegally if he leaves his ground too soon. The new wording put the responsibility fair and square on the batsman. This reflected the fact that sympathies had shifted towards the bowler. The wording of the Law also, however, tries to preclude deliberate entrapment, stating that the crucial period of liability extends only 'until the instant when the bowler *would normally have been expected to release the ball*', not until he actually does release it. Thus it requires umpires not to allow bowlers to entrap the batsman by deliberate delay in removing the bails.

9

TRYING NOT TO WIN AND NOT TRYING

'The common criminal is a bad man but at least he is, as it were, a conditional good man.'

G. K. Chesterton

In his novel *The Man Who Was Thursday*, G. K. Chesterton writes:

We say that the dangerous criminal now is the educated criminal. We say that the most dangerous criminal now is the entirely lawless modern philosopher. Compared to him, burglars and bigamists are essentially moral men; my heart goes out to them. They accept the essential idea of man; they merely seek it wrongly. Thieves respect property. They merely wish the property to become their property . . . But philosophers dislike property as property; they wish to destroy the very idea of personal possession. Bigamists respect marriage, or they would not go through the highly ceremonial and even ritualistic formality of bigamy. But philosophers despise marriage as marriage. Murderers respect human life; they merely wish to attain a greater fullness of human life in themselves, by the sacrifice of what seem to them to be lesser lives. But philosophers hate life itself, their own as much as other people's . . . The common criminal is a bad man but at least he is, as it were, a conditional good man. He says that if only a certain obstacle be removed – say a wealthy uncle – he is then prepared to accept the universe and to praise God. He is a reformer, but not an anarchist. He wishes to cleanse the edifice, but not to destroy it. But the evil philosopher is not trying to alter things, but to annihilate them.

Something similar is to be said for the distinction between corruption and common-or-garden cheating in sport. The former – the revolutionary, the nihilist – attacks the whole concept of fair play, 'destroying the edifice' of the game, whereas the machinations of the latter are a matter of adjusting the arrangements of a particular game, like a burglar who has no objection to property as such, but merely wants to re-allocate a small element of it. No doubt there are psychopaths for whom the knowledge of right and wrong is deeply repressed, or perhaps has never been developed. But even they have, I suspect, expelled their hazy, unformed beginnings of knowledge in order to make their corruption tenable to themselves.

The person who throws a game, or part of one, primarily for an advantage that lies outside the game (money, backhanders, brown envelopes) – though there may well be other more secret gains in the form of excitement, secrecy and power – puts the whole activity under suspicion. What looks like a transparent, authentic contest, with evident striving, is undermined. Spectators, unable to know whom to trust, are deceived about the integrity of the activity. Even honest errors (like wides bowled early in a Test, or matches there for the winning that are inexplicably lost) start to fall under suspicion. Ordinary followers say: 'I don't know what I'm watching nowadays.' They are disillusioned.

Moreover, team-mates who are not in the plan are betrayed. While the majority are eager to win, and to do as well as they can, the corrupt one(s) are conniving to lose, or to produce a partial outcome that is against their team's interests, but in the interests of corrupt bookmakers and their own bank balance. The opposition too are precluded from properly winning, deprived of the satisfaction of having earned their now tarnished win. It has not been eleven versus eleven but eleven plus one versus eleven minus one.

Such activity, akin to Chesterton's nihilism, reduces sport to second-rate play-acting. I suppose sport-theatre of this kind is acceptable if there is no attempt to hide the pretence, as in some forms of wrestling that blatantly stage a sort of morality play, with 'heels' (pantomime villains) and 'daddies' (goodies), and with pre-scripted plots and outcomes; the heel duly gets his comeuppance. There are exhibition events too, as used to be staged in basketball by the Harlem Globetrotters, in which the aim was to demonstrate eye-catching basketball skills, but in which a central point of sport was, in this case harmlessly, set aside. A parallel example is the masterclass – Brian Lara showing how he could hit the same delivery safely in a variety of different directions by minute shifts in hand and body position, or Daniel Barenboim showing how a Beethoven piano sonata might be approached and performed.

But purposely trying not to win destroys the fabric of the activity. Chesterton quotes the end of Alexander Pope's *The Dunciad*:

> Lo! thy dread Empire, Chaos, is restored;
> Light dies before thine uncreating word:
> Thy hand, great Anarch, lets the curtain fall;
> And universal darkness buries all.

* * *

Some complain that the penalties for the three Australians in the sandpaper affair were too lenient. However, the basic offence was common-or-garden cheating of a kind that has been rife throughout cricket's history, though not usually so blatantly. Vic Marks, cricket writer and former England player, asks how different today's ball-tampering is from that of the sixties to eighties, when 'the ball almost shredded your fingers when you caught it'. First-class umpires in the past (many of whom had been bowlers in their younger days) saw it as par for the course.

Ball-tampering is not corruption. The most severe punishment imposed by ICC in the Sandpaper case was, in accordance with the customary tariff, a one-Test ban. Only afterwards were the three men given much longer bans, from all cricket, by their own board. Perhaps it would have been better if the rationale for this severity – so much for the tampering, so much for the lying, so much for getting a junior player to do the deed, so much for the long-term boorishness of the team as a whole, and so much for harming Australia's self-image – had been made explicit at the time.

During the Ashes series of 2019, it was interesting that, when the three men returned to the team, Steve Smith, who had a prodigiously successful series, scoring 774 runs at an average of 110.57, received much less booing from English crowds than David Warner, whose fortunes were radically different (95 runs at 9.5). It seemed that English crowds were more willing to congratulate success than sympathise with failure. History favours winners.

As for corruption, no one in my time ever dreamed of throwing a match. But then the temptations were not there. I never heard of players being approached by bookmakers for illicit information.

* * *

Corruption in sport involves deliberate failing, an attack on the credibility of the whole enterprise. Is there a relationship between this and other forms of not really trying?

It would be an understatement to describe match-fixing as 'not trying'. The latter does not amount to corruption, in fact it is usually quite different, but it may lead people to believe that not minding, even indifference about winning or losing, is more mature than ordinary trying. It may also result from such a belief.

After my South London talk on the point of sport I had a conversation with a young, keen and, from what I gathered, talented footballer. He vehemently agreed with my suggestion that not trying might be acting in the wrong spirit. In fact, he thought I was too mealy-mouthed about it. He couldn't stand it if a team took their foot off the pedal against his side. He would rather be defeated 10–0 with the opposition playing at their best than 2–1 when they deliberately eased up. Such behaviour really got to him. He felt patronised. Also, he said, if they behaved like this, he and his team couldn't use the experience to learn. This young man had strong views about the spirit of sport.

In January 1973, I was invited to join Kent as a guest player on their short tour of the West Indies. The previous summer, they had won the 40-over Sunday league, and were to play matches with these rules in the main Caribbean cricketing locations. They needed some 'ringers' since Mike Denness, Derek Underwood and Alan Knott were all touring India with the MCC. Naturally, I was delighted to join them.

Colin Cowdrey, Kent's captain, was unable to go on the tour until the second week. In the first we had played matches in Jamaica, Trinidad, Tobago and Barbados. We had done our best, against keen and skilful opposition, but had lost more than we had won. One match soon after Cowdrey joined us was against Guyana, a strong side led by future West Indies captain, Clive Lloyd. The pitch was flat and grassless, and the outfield fast. After 20 overs, the score was something like 90 for 2, with Test batsmen Alvin Kallicharran and Lloyd at the crease. We had done reasonably well. At this point Colin decided that, this being a so-called 'friendly' match, he would put on non-specialist bowlers. We didn't exactly 'give' them runs, but we didn't try too hard to stop them. Not surprisingly, when the so-called 'joke' bowlers were on, the ball kept sailing out of the ground. When we tried to peg them back with regular bowlers, we did little better.

Guyana piled up 223 for 6, a big score for those days. When we batted, they bowled at their best and we were beaten by 63 runs.

I felt critical of this 'friendly' business, this 'almost giving' of runs. Not all gifts are positive (the German word 'Gift' means 'poison'). I felt that by not trying our hardest we diminished the game. It meant that we didn't fully lose – after all, we hadn't fully tried – and Guyana didn't fully win because their opponents had held back. We were not exactly Trojan horses, but as the young footballer implied, there was something Trojan in these gifts.

Of course, there are contexts in which such gestures *are* appropriate. If a men's team is playing against schoolboys, they may not feel free to bowl with full force. When I was thirteen, and small for my age, my father's club side was one short at Malden Wanderers, a strong Surrey club team. Batting at number ten, I came in to help save the game, surviving the last few minutes (perhaps half an hour?) against a leg-spinner who had played for Kent Second XI and a man called Harry Edney, who started his run-up with a curiously debonair flourish of arms and legs, which I remember to this day, and bowled fast by my standards. I learned sixty-odd years later that some of their players were aggrieved at my presence because they could not bowl flat out against this small boy. Now I can see their point. Stephen Chalke tells me a story of his team's Barbadian fast bowler bowling six off breaks to a schoolboy number eleven in the last over of a match; the boy safely blocked them all without difficulty. In friendly cricket would you crowd a youngster? Or ease up? What would your fair dinkum Aussie think about this? Or the solitary Yorkshireman in your team? And would it happen in league cricket?

Again, when people are playing for fun, or only for fun, it may be imperative to make sure everyone gets a turn with bat or ball, whatever the match. If you're winning a game easily, you might give a lesser bowler a chance, or promote a young batsman in the order.

In some friendly games the art of captaincy consists in manoeuvring the game to be as close to a tie as possible.

But I thought Cowdrey got it wrong. These players were far from being schoolboys, and far from needing any help from us. I imagine that the crowd too were not deceived. I think the 'generosity' was in fact misguided, verging on the patronising.

Not trying may, then, go against the spirit of sport, against the grain.

Remembering this made me wonder further about the story of Cowdrey's extraordinary handshake with Jeff Thomson, when he came into bat in the Perth Test match. Cowdrey, you may remember, was forty-one. Thomson was as fast a bowler as anyone in the world. The pitch was bouncy. When I told a friend this story, he said: 'Cowdrey must have been taking the piss.' Another asked: 'Was he trying to disarm Thommo's macho aggression?' Or was he too eager to please, too apprehensive about ridicule?

Was he? Or was he a sort of naive holy man, like Alyosha in Dostoyevsky's *Brothers Karamazov*, or Prince Myshkin in his novel *The Idiot*; a fool according to the sceptical reckoning of the world at large, but possibly also a man who tends to see good everywhere and is too selfless to feel afraid? I have come up against this question earlier in this book, with my psychoanalytic colleague who asked: 'But why would you even *think* of doing such things?' Am I too suspicious? Are they, Christina and Colin, not 'too good to be true', not people role-playing goodness or playing a psychological game (a game unlikely to succeed, I would have thought, with the Australian fast bowler), but simply good? Have I, have we become cynical, have we lost a belief in simple goodness of the kind shown by the excellent Sri Lankan charity run by Kushil Gunasekera, which has no embarrassment in calling itself the 'Foundation of Goodness'? I'm reminded of the renaming of another excellent charity, this one in the UK: the 'Students Partnership Worldwide' became 'Restless Development', acknowledging in its new title that restlessness may be a driver to good action, and implying that we should not rest in this exhausting task, nor should our swords sleep in our hands. The new name implies a more complex and indeed more restless world than their Sri Lankan counterpart. As John Major put it: 'We live in a world in which cynicism elevates the shabby and the tawdry, and sneers at the naivety of the honourable and the honest'. He sees scoffing at the spirit of cricket as an extra reason for upholding it.

However, even if there are rare Myshkins in the world, people of open-hearted simplicity and guilelessness, at least sometimes the phenomenon of not trying goes against the spirit of sport. Some sport-haters may argue that competitive sport is itself a second-rate activity, that it betrays in its acolytes a failure to grow up. One patient, having just found out about my previous career on the cricket field, asked me: 'How can a mature woman like me learn from a latency-level boy like you, who's spent your life playing juvenile games with other little boys?'

However that may be, my view is that avoiding head-on competitiveness (in sport and at times in life) may itself be a sign of immaturity. It may, for example, be done to protect oneself against the risk of real loss by refusing to take things seriously. Or perhaps it is a matter of sneering at people who do? One professional cricketer would after being dismissed return to the dressing room whistling insouciantly, as if his dismissal was of the smallest importance to him. His team-mates did mind, and his indifference conveyed the message that he was above minding, that minding was in fact small-minded!

One giveaway for such an attitude is the smirk. I see it in some political leaders. They play the fool, are bumptious, even buffoons. In 2004, Boris Johnson published a novel entitled *Seventy-Two Virgins*. The hero of the book, Roger Barlow, is a 'bicycling MP known for tousled hair, classical allusions and flapping shirt-tails . . . To a man like Roger Barlow, the whole world just seemed to be a complicated joke . . . everything was always up for grabs, capable of dispute; and religion, laws, principle, custom – these were nothing but sticks from the wayside to support our faltering step.' He writes of his character's 'startling political and spiritual nihilism'.

This self-portrait – I think it safe to say, at least of a Johnson before the shocking seriousness of his near-death experience of coronavirus illness – is a disturbing example of someone whose emptiness is covered by turning everything into a joke, by becoming a parody of oneself. Strangely, others are taken in, and taken over, by such attitudes. The reaction to him often involves a smirk. 'Oh, that's just Boris,' people say, with an inane grin on their own faces. We may be inclined to do so ourselves. Donald Trump's supporters excuse him in similar ways: 'That's what Trump is like,' say his supporters, excusing the latest piece of crassness, paranoia or self-importance. And as they excuse him, these followers, too, smirk.

Johnson became prime minister in July 2019. In September John Major was interviewed on the radio, after Johnson had threatened to 'prorogue' Parliament if that were what it would take to get the UK out of the European Union by 31 October 2019; vowing to 'do or die, come what may'. Major regarded this idea of proroguing as offending against the central pillar of parliamentary democracy, namely, that the government should be open to challenge from Parliament. My point here is that Major did not once refer to Johnson as 'Boris'. In quite a long interview he repeatedly called him 'Mr Johnson', a form of address that in an earlier period of English history would have been how the middle classes spoke about tradesmen. But I thought Major's main aim was to avoid the smirk factor.

So why do people respond with such excusing grins? I suspect because they too would in their dream worlds like to be able to say whatever comes into their heads, to be exempt from considering the real world, to be empty enough to assume that others will fall in with their imperious demands. In Mozart's opera *Don Giovanni* the 'hero' seduced women of all classes – '640 in Italy, 231 in Germany, 100 in

France, a mere 91 in Turkey; but in Spain, 1,003,' his servant Leporello says of him. This precise and egregious enumeration creates a smirk factor, disguising the cruelty. But why did the women fall for him? Might it be that they too wished for easy sensual gratification? Or did they all have fantasies of rescuing him from a life of debauchery?

In *The Portrait of a Lady*, Henry James describes the obnoxious Gilbert Osmond, a man whose manner is to set himself above ordinary human ambitions, to be superior to ordinary striving (though underneath this mask, his striving is Machiavellian). He is languid, with sophisticated tastes, especially in art. The whole act is a sham, whereby he succeeds in deceiving the rich, innocent and high-minded heroine of the novel, Isabel Archer, into a loveless marriage. James writes of Osmond's villa: 'The windows of the ground floor, as you saw them from the piazza, were, in their noble proportions, extremely architectural; but their function seemed less to offer communication with the world than to defy the world to look in.' And of the man himself: 'Osmond, in his way, was admirable; he had the advantage of an acquired habit. It was not that of succeeding but it was something almost as good – that of not attempting.' James has 'looked in', behind the 'noble proportions'.

10

NOT ONLY THE PLAYERS

'What hurt was a new reaction. A huge roar of delight went up as my ball went down into the sand. Hundreds actually stood there clapping.'

Peter Thomson, Australian golfer

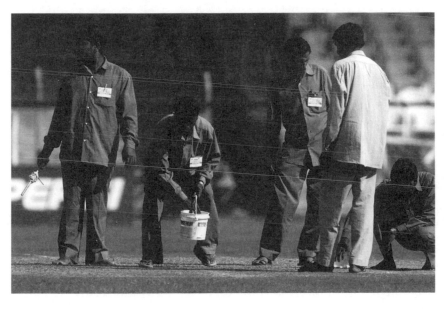

In August 2019, MCC sent an email to members in advance of the Test at Lord's against Australia: 'The Spirit of Cricket should live in all aspects of your time at the Ground: welcome the players to Lord's warmly, treat each other and the Club's staff with respect and celebrate all that is good about MCC.'

Here is another expansion or instantiation of what might be involved in acting according to the spirit of cricket. This one is addressed not to players, but to members. And though the Spirit of Cricket Preamble is directed primarily at the players, it applies more broadly: to coaches and back-room staff, to umpires, parents, administrators, groundsmen; to the media; even (in an attenuated sense) to spectators.

Individuals are inevitably shaped by and react to their social environment. Society affects children and the adults they become. The standard of behaviour of, and expected from, cricketers, as in other systems, is bound to reflect changes in large-scale social attitudes. Sportsmen/women are subject to projections from the man and woman in the street.

Of course, the reverse is true too: individuals influence the broader attitudes. Remember W. H. Auden's famous phrase in his obituary poem about Freud's impact – 'to us he is no more a person now but a whole climate of opinion'.

Global climate changes produce a range of regional shifts in weather patterns. Metaphorically, in cricketing terms, New Zealand have responded to boorishness by a reversion to values (especially love of the game).

Not that these values have ever gone away. A widely received idea is that money eats away at sportspeople's values. However, my own experience as a professional cricketer was that playing for money did not infringe on this mentality. In one of my first games for Middlesex, I dropped a catch at deep square leg off Fred Titmus. Not only that, but I deflected the ball over the boundary for six. I was mortified and also nervous about the reaction. But when I apologised to Fred, he said, with genuine kindliness: 'It's not so much the dropping that bothers me. It was you palming it over for six!' This was a more humorous and less resentful attitude than many to be found in club cricket or in everyday life.

Professional cricketers love cricket – though loving someone or something doesn't preclude hating it at times. ('*Odi et amo*': I hate (her) and I love (her), the poet Catullus famously wrote). One of the pleasures after retirement in meeting old cricketing colleagues is the depth of that love, which is reflected in detailed shared memories of incidents from forty or fifty years ago, often recollected with warmth and humour. The love outweighs the rest.

This passion for the game did not, of course, rule out our occasional relief when heavy rain stopped play, putting anxiety on the back burner. In rhyming slang, sometimes called 'cockney slang' as it began in the East End of London, 'duke' means 'rain' (via the 'Duke of Spain'), and really heavy rain was 'Archduke'. I've been in dressing rooms where Archduke was celebrated as a visitation by benign weather gods, providing welcome respite from the need for hard endeavour, and from the risk of exposure and failure.

Professionalism may turn play into work, with its onus on duty and anxiety. So much depends on success not only for one's well-being and reputation but also for getting another contract. It is also possible that the proliferation of coaches and of computer-based feedback has led modern cricketers to be more wrapped up in issues of their personal technique than in the more haphazard environment of several decades ago.

The Spirit of Cricket slogan nudges us towards a congenial, collegial attitude, a reminder not to let our passion be contaminated and weighed down by earnestness, ruthlessness or a self-protective indifference, elements of which are conveyed by the values and expectations of the wider public.

* * *

Cricket crowds have changed. They are more militant and collective in their hostilities, possibly more mindless. Recently, short-term excitement levels have been increasingly hyped up, most noisily and tempestuously in India, and in T20 cricket, by loud music, flame-throwing machines, flashing lights, fireworks, and cheerleaders prancing about in front of the stands. The manic atmosphere evoked fires up tribalism and boorishness, as well as festive good spirits. But crowd changes began long ago.

Surrey and England cricketer Micky Stewart remembers 'watching a [football] match in the early '50s at Stamford Bridge, when the Chelsea full-back Stan Willemse kicked Stanley Matthews, and the crowd booed him. His own crowd. But twenty years later, when Ron Harris did the same to George Best, kicking him out of the game in the first twenty minutes, they cheered. Times had changed.'

In the Melbourne Test of 1954–5, the England dressing room was outraged by, and highly critical of, a new crowd phenomenon: as England's batsmen sought to survive at the end of a day's play, fans banged empty beer cans on the concrete terracing in protest at their slow scoring. Australian golfer Peter Thomson, who was a guest in the dressing room at the time, later discussed the players' reaction with Colin Cowdrey.

In his autobiography, Cowdrey describes Thomson's recalling of his own shock during the play-off in a recent US golf tournament. He and his American opponent arrived at the seventeenth tee all square: '"I saw my iron shot catch the wind, veer fractionally off-course, hit the top of a bunker and then slowly run back into the sand. What hurt," he said, was a new reaction. "A huge roar of delight went up as my ball went down into the sand. Hundreds actually stood there clapping."' Thomson told Cowdrey: '"Your players should be clear-minded about . . . this kind of alien reaction."'

Thomson's point was not only that crowds were 'not always going to lean over backwards to show generosity to visitors'; he also saw consequences for players. His advice to the England cricket team was to learn to live with it. Cowdrey takes this further: 'The lesson for cricket is obvious. Its players too must care far more and take on collective responsibility. It matters that we seek the best, avoiding pettiness, cut out bad language, control temperament, spare time for members and be part of the club's social functions.'

Cowdrey jumps from a fact about unseemly and ungenerous crowd behaviour to a requirement for players to become well-behaved schoolboys. I suppose there is truth in what he writes: if players did more in these directions, hostility might, just, be attenuated (though not by much, I suspect).

My point is the simpler one, that crowds too behave in ways that are 'not cricket'. They have become more tribal, more partisan. Australian crowds swear at England players and supporters; and English crowds do the same to Australians. More now than sixty or seventy years ago, they gloat over others' misfortunes and take pleasure in – even applaud – the failings of opponents. When in 2019 Steve Smith was felled at Lord's by Jofra Archer's bouncer, a few in the crowd cheered as he collapsed.

I would say that the clubs have more responsibility than the players for curbing such excesses. There are risks in the societal transformations that have resulted in us British becoming less phlegmatic, less repressed. Hence MCC's letter to members, underlining their responsibilities in terms of the spirit of the game (though I'm inclined to believe that the issue is not particular to cricket; it's relevant to communal life in general).

I'm not advocating vapidity among crowds. Like players, crowds may be hard but fair, cutting but humorous. In 2019 – nine days after the extraordinary last day at Headingley, when Australian bowler Nathan Lyon, given a perfect chance to run out number eleven batsman, Jack Leach, with England needing 2 to win – the crowd at the next Test (at Manchester) roared delightedly every time the bowler caught the ball when it was tossed to him during an over. Lyon looked less amused.

Two comments directed at me on the field come to mind. One was at Trent Bridge, during the match against Australia in 1977.

I was wearing under my England cap a small skullcap, the forerunner of the helmets that became customary within a year. While I was running between the wickets, cap and skull protector fell off. A wag in the crowd shouted: 'Why don't you stick it on with a six-inch nail, Brearley?' The other was in 1979. Four years earlier, Mike Denness had captained England in Australia and had had a poor run of form, as I was having then. A man called out from 'the Hill' at Sydney Cricket Ground: 'Breely, you make Denness look like Bradman.' These were not kindly comments, but they were amusing; they were more like family teasing than undifferentiated rubbishing or jeering.

The partisanship of crowds may be admirable and stimulating. They are entitled to be robust, which may include booing to express disapproval of certain player behaviour – though I think too that this booing quickly degenerates into mindlessness. I disliked the booing of Sachithra Senanayake at Edgbaston when he ran Jos Buttler out. Crowds are liable to be cruel.

I wrote above that the spirit of cricket applies to spectators, to crowds, in an *attenuated* sense. Why so? I think it is a matter of what the different groups owe to cricket. People playing the game, especially but not only professionally, owe much to its institutions, its clubs and its traditions. In return we have duties and debts to cricket. Much the same applies to people with other roles in the game – coaches, umpires and so on. The closer the links, and the more employment is a factor, the more these reciprocal responsibilities apply. Cricket clubs and organisations, each within its sphere, hear charges against players and others for bringing the club and/or the game into disrepute. They will at the same time offer advice and support to the individuals concerned if a complaint is made against them. Bringing the game into disrepute is the obverse of behaving within its spirit.

There are parallels in many fields. As a psychoanalyst I could be charged with bringing the profession or my professional organisation into disrepute. Again, this organisation will clear me if the complaint is false, malicious or unproven. There is a spirit of proper behaviour due to the discipline and to our institutions, as well as, of course, proper behaviour owed to patients. Both organisations – in cricket and in psychoanalysis – have duties in relation to me, to protect me from slanders and vexatious harassment, or alternatively to discipline me if the complaint is found to be correct.

In cricket, the more peripheral and intermittent the link with the game the less the spirit of cricket as such applies. For the occasional spectator, there is little that is specific to the game. For him, behaving in a proper manner is largely a matter of following ordinary social norms and customs. Apart from rules relating to the specificity of sport in general (not to trespass on the field of play, for example), what remains for cricket *per se* fades into mere matters of etiquette – to considerations of what constitutes appropriate clothing, for example, or what the customary limits are in displaying disgruntlement or excitement.

It follows from this that, among spectators, club members have more obligations than the anonymous man or woman paying for their ticket and dropping in on a game. Members may appropriately be arraigned by the club for letting the club down. One member of the MCC was – rightly – evicted from the pavilion during the Test against Australia mentioned above for verbally abusing Smith as, at the end of his courageous and skilful innings of 92, he walked back through the Long Room.

* * *

Do those making judgements about cricketers and other sportsmen have a duty to act and speak in accordance with this proper spirit? Judging calls for fairness – for justice arrived at with accuracy of differentiation, for justice tempered with mercy. As novelist John Steinbeck puts it in his novel *Sweet Thursday*: if the small-town policeman is a good constable, when presented with weeping little boys and girls who have 'lifted' small items from sweet shops, he 'gives them a sense of mercy-in-justice without injuring the dignity of the law'.

There are bound to be differences between players and commentators. The former long to be understood and loved; the latter seek stories, dramas, some of them unfavourable to the players. And criticism is often deserved; it may even be learned from.

But criticism may descend to baying for blood: it's not (in my view) within the spirit of cricket to propose life bans for all those involved, however slightly, with corruption. That would be like hanging boys for stealing sheep.

It may be that those in favour of draconian punishments are in that very attitude putting cricket on a pedestal of perfection that's unrealistic and ultimately inhuman. They have the idea that cricket should be such a pure, clean area that everyone involved is to behave better than anywhere else. I suggest that purity is a dubious virtue, tending towards fundamentalism. It's true that if we set our ethical standards too low, we tolerate a descent into contempt and even incitement to mutual hostility. But if we put them too high, we risk hypocrisy and disillusion, and may find other outlets for the less worthy feelings we have tried to get rid of. (I do see that, without demanding impossible standards of purity, it would be logically consistent to expect more from cricketers – and psychoanalysts for that matter – in their boundaried contexts than from all of us in the multifarious, messier living of a life.)

Like politicians, some media pundits would do well to consider the possibility that their vituperative language becomes an incitement to action by sections of the population, to behaviour that goes beyond what the writers or politicians would themselves engage in.

As an ex-player and (part-time) writer on cricket, I have had to reckon with various questions about the spirit in which I write. Am I tempted to disparage the current game? Do I subtly or otherwise belittle aspects of it to build up myself or the values or standards of my day? I think the answer is yes, I am tempted to do that. It is all too easy to become, for example, exasperated with what I sometimes see as unduly defensive field-settings among Test captains and bowlers, or with unduly attacking mindsets of many batsmen. If I give way to these temptations I become like commentators from previous generations who in the spirit of 'the good old days' disparaged us, enjoying putting the boot in, a tendency that is both unfair and tedious.

From time to time, English players feel – rightly or wrongly – that there is a certain *Schadenfreude* among commentators in this country. Do the media in general prefer England to fail? I don't know the answer to this question. We may lean too far in blaming or disparaging ourselves, at a national or local level. Or we may swing from exaggerated praise to condemnation and blame, whether from disappointment or from the pursuit of a dramatic story. But fair-mindedness is also valuable in itself, and a necessary counter to tribalism.

Personally, I'm aware of certain resentments, which I try to keep out of sight, even to modify. For instance, it is still painful for me to remember that I never scored a Test century. When England's opener, Dominic Sibley, scored his first, at Cape Town in 2020, he was naturally overjoyed. Ex-players commented on how he would remember the moment for the rest of his life; how important it was, a marker of acceptance at this level; a token to himself and others that he belonged as a Test batsman. Hearing this, even thinking of this as I write, I am aware of traces of envy. I am pleased for him, but having never scored one hurts on two grounds: one is that I didn't get that reassurance; the second that if I had managed to convert the 91 I scored in Mumbai in 1977 to three figures, I think I would have been more likely to score another.

I learned something else from watching Sibley's plucky and determined innings and from noticing my own mixed reactions. He is not the sort of player one would, especially at first sight, see as an automatic Test batsman. He is not elegant or fluent, not classical in technique. Looking back on some notes I wrote about him at the time, I realised that I'd mis-written his name: Dominic 'Sibling', I called him. So there it was – sibling rivalry, emerging straight from my unconscious! Clearly, I saw this gritty, courageous and potentially successful Test opener as a parallel case to myself. By contrast, when in the following Test match, at Port Elizabeth, the more obviously talented and even younger Ollie Pope scored *his* first hundred, I didn't feel envy. The difference is that Pope bats at another level, more assured, deft, more complete a player, already more accomplished. I did of course feel envious of batsmen like Sachin Tendulkar or Brian Lara; but this was a more distant, less galling kind of feeling than I would feel for a batsman more or less like myself. As philosopher David Hume said, we are more likely to be resentfully envious of those near us in status than of those whose place in life is far removed from our own.

I have to struggle with this kind of carping, painful, sibling-type rivalry. I discount it and usually don't mention it. It is not a pleasant characteristic.

There are also alarm calls, but of a different kind, when I focus on the options and decisions taken by cricket captains. When I watch or think about a game of cricket or a passage of play I cannot but think tactically and psychologically. My whole experience is ingrained with such considerations. If I were to express too many of these thought processes, or simply describe them in detail, I might come across as over-critical of what current captains are or aren't doing. This is at times true; but much of it is a matter of fascination with the topic – with what one might try the next ball, next over, next session; what might unsettle a batsman, with questions like: 'When is it best to take an attacking risk?' 'When to consolidate or try to keep control?'

In all these areas there are challenges for the writer/commentator. Can I be open to modern mindsets and to the shifting sands of fashion as well as to my own take on the game? Can I allow myself not to know, while being aware of the momentary moves of my mind towards condescension or inferiority?

We have mental and emotional hinterlands, all of us. For some these are and remain hidden. Others struggle with theirs. And however erratic and self-serving they may be, struggling to give houseroom to our unworthy thoughts and feelings is for many of us necessary if we are to become more self-aware, if we are to enlarge the availability of the hinterland.

One final example relating to the media. Broadcasters need to behave with integrity when it comes to DRS and the use of cameras in general. There is a possibility for a broadcaster to be selective in what to show, depending on the allegiances of his or her core audience; and there is also the (slight) risk of technology being set up in a way that gives a distorted impression of the evidence available to umpires.

* * *

The spirit of cricket applies to the groundsman, from whom we should also expect integrity as well as know-how. His (or 'her', I suppose I should add) job is to make the best possible pitch, one on which to different degrees the varied skills of the game will be given a more or less balanced chance.

In the 2019 County Championship, Somerset needed to win the last match of the season at Taunton against Essex. They were later found guilty of unfairly doctoring the pitch, making one that would, with good weather, have helped their own side and guaranteed a result in a short time. They had 12 points deducted for the start of the following season.

The groundsman is often on a hiding to nothing. If the pitch is flat, and batting is dominant in the match, he is criticised for pitches being 'too good' – though this phrase indicates that the quality of goodness is measured by how things are for batsmen! If bowlers are on top, he is condemned for imbalance in the opposite direction.

Groundsmen are often wrongly advised, and then wrongly blamed. For example, ground authorities may be over-concerned to ensure that matches go the distance (so as not to lose revenue). They may be over-anxious about being criticised. Groundsmen are liable to be wrongly blamed when one or both sides play badly, or wrongly praised if they play extremely well, on a given pitch; or when weather intervenes to make the ball do more (or less) than might have been expected.

For the Test match at Lord's between England and Ireland in July 2019, each team was out for one very low score – England for 85 in their first innings, Ireland for 38 in their second. Both these innings took place under heavy cloud cover and in humid conditions that 'greened' up the pitch and favoured seam bowlers. When the sun shone, by contrast, Ireland were at one stage 131 for 2, and England 171 for 1. Jack Leach, England's number eleven, until this innings averaging 4 with the bat during the current season, scored 92 as night-watchman. It's hard to believe it can have been such a bad pitch, but England captain Joe Root slammed the groundsman, saying the pitch was too friendly to seam bowling.

Groundsmen are, moreover, sometimes got at, usually by home players, coaches and administrators, all wanting to influence the kind of pitch he prepares, especially for big matches. Usually these pressures are aimed at unduly favouring the home team.

In the week following the Ireland match, Australia won the first Ashes Test, at Edgbaston. There was then speculation about the kind of pitch England needed if they were to have their best chance of coming back in the series, specifically in the next match, also at Lord's, nine days later. Commentators implied that the situation was touchy, since Root would now, as a result of his recent comments, find it hard to ask for a pitch that would favour seam bowling.

Such comments make an assumption that goes against the spirit of cricket. They imply that England, or any home side, whether through its captain or its coaches, have a right to influence the pitch for an upcoming match. To my mind, unless the request is for the best possible pitch for cricket – that is, for conditions that are likely to provide, within the range of traditional English (and Lord's) pitches, a good-enough balance between bat and ball, and between different types of bowler – such a presumption is unethical. The word that comes to mind is 'fixing' – fixing pitches as opposed to fixing matches, but still fixing. The making of pitches should be for the expert, the groundsman, not for the sides that are to be tried and tested on that pitch. Like a defendant in a law court, the home side should have no say in the conditions under which the testing takes place, unless they can rightly complain that impropriety has occurred or is likely to occur.

The groundsman is responsible for the pitch. He is the expert. He is also required to be disinterested in his preparation. Similarly, before play and during the match he has a duty to answer questions put to him by players from either side in a neutral and honest way. It would be against the spirit of the game for him to be more forthcoming to the home captain than to the visiting captain. The groundsman should be as unbiased as the umpire.

For games played on artificial pitches covered with matting, he should be meticulous in ensuring that the mat is stretched to exactly the same degree whichever side is going to be batting or bowling. In the 1950s and '60s, when matting pitches were still in use at some venues for first-class matches overseas, visiting players used to complain that this was not always the case; the more loosely the matting was stretched, the more purchase bowlers who spin or cut the ball were able to get.

In 2012, at Mumbai, the (natural grass) pitch for the Second Test between India and England took spin sharply from day one. Against expectation, and despite losing the toss, Kevin Pietersen, with one of his most brilliant innings, and Alastair Cook both scored centuries that enabled England to win, thus drawing level in the series. With the next Test to be at Eden Gardens, Kolkata, India's captain M. S. Dhoni got in touch with the groundsman there, Prabhir Mukherjee, to try to persuade him to make a pitch that would turn even more.

Mukherjee, then eighty-three years old, had been in charge of the Eden Gardens pitch for twenty-seven years. He was not one to kow-tow. On an earlier occasion he had ordered Mike Atherton off the square as he did not have the appropriate accreditation. Now, he told Dhoni it was none of his business. When BCCI hastily (and disgracefully) tried to remove him from his post, and put another man in charge for the match, he was outspoken. 'Immoral' was his word, both for Dhoni's attempt to pressurise him and for the board's proposal to dismiss or demote him. He was clear: he would put his trust in the tried and tested methods that had served him and the venue well for so many years.

The same should be said to any England spokesman, whether captain, coach or administrator, who tries to 'nobble' a ground authority, either by directly bending the ear of the groundsman, or through other channels. And 'immoral' implies: against the spirit of cricket.

During my stint as captain of Middlesex, who were (and are) tenants of MCC, the owners of Lord's, the then groundsman, Jim Fairbrother, was forbidden to speak to me. The issue, as I saw it, was that MCC had instructed him to make pitches for county matches that were guaranteed not to 'break up', that is, they were not to crumble from being dry or worn as had traditionally been the case late in the season. Along with other players, I was convinced that some such instruction had led to pitches starting off damp even after prolonged dry weather. If you scratched them with your spikes, a dark brown colour was disclosed just beneath the light brown surface. The outcome was that they suited medium-pace bowlers more than quick ones and took little or no spin towards the end of the match. They got easier for batting as the match went on. I complained. There was nothing personal in it, and my complaint was directed at the orders from above more than their recipient. Probably I became too heated in my exasperation. But my point was a fair one, that such pitches make it relatively easy to stay in, harder to play shots; and lead to defensive field-placings – in other words to boring cricket with a high likelihood of draws. It was not so much that the policy was hurting Middlesex (which it was, as our strength lay in our spinners and quick bowlers rather than in medium-pace bowlers). It was more that it spoiled the contest and blunted many of the game's most interesting skills. But it's true that the situation was particularly galling to us as our competitors, at least those that owned their grounds, were able to make pitches that suited their own strengths and were more likely to produce results. I can see that Fairbrother was put in an invidious position; but something of the spirit of Mukherjee would have been welcome.

* * *

Most games of golf have no referee or umpire. Cricket, with its multiple modes of dismissal, and its call for diverse and discriminating judgements, requires them. I remember a playground tennis-ball game of cricket when I was eleven or so. A large wastebasket served as the stumps. I had been batting for a while, probably already for too long. Someone bowled me an off break. I knew the rules, and padded up. The ball hit me outside the line of the wicket (i.e. basket), so I could not, according to the Laws of cricket at that time, properly be adjudged lbw. In lieu of umpires, negotiations had to be conducted by batsman and fielders. I knew I was not, technically, out. The bowler could see that the ball was going to hit the basket. I remember refusing, petulantly, to give up the bat. I had been too clever by half. Why did I not simply try to hit the ball, as anyone else would have done? And why behave so fretfully, fractiously and self-righteously, just because I *knew* I was right? Remembering the episode, I feel ashamed again. That boy has not entirely disappeared from my personality.

Going up one small step from playground cricket to those unregulated friendly matches, even pick-up games, where no umpires have been enlisted, members of the batting side often stand in. These player-umpires are expected to do their best to switch from being partisan to a proper neutrality. One was told by his captain: 'The trouble with you and your umpiring is you're too fair!'

Umpires are as important as players in creating the right spirit.

I have mentioned one outrageous attempt by umpires to cheat, asking the home captain, Imran Khan, which of the opposition batsmen he would like them to 'see off'. At high levels of the game, umpires, like players, are liable, occasionally, to be offered enticements from bookmakers and gamblers, both for information and for more insidious interference in outcomes. Clearly, if umpires go along with any of this, they become corrupt judges, acting both against the spirit, and in some instances the Laws, of cricket.

Like judges, too, they may also allow personal elements to get in the way of truthfulness, whether deliberately or unconsciously. What the game needs is umpires who understand the game and the players, who make good or good-enough decisions, and who act with total impartiality.

At the highest level, the Decision Review System has made some difference, for the better in my view. First and most importantly, it provides public evidence for what has actually happened. Players and umpires find it satisfying that truth is (usually, at least) served, and injustices undone.

Second, restriction on the number of unsuccessful reviews permitted calls for an honesty and avoidance of wishful thinking by batsmen, fielding teams and captains alike, since with each review they risk losing chances to ask for reviews later on. In 2019, Australia's error of this kind directly lost them the Headingley Test match, since their wasteful challenge during the final stages of the extraordinary climax, when the ball had obviously pitched outside leg stump against Jack Leach, meant they had no appeal left to challenge a bad not-out decision when, with England nine wickets down, and two runs from victory, Nathan Lyon straightened the ball along the line of middle-and-leg stump against Stokes.

DRS thus focuses the players' minds in new ways. Accuracy of perception is not just a matter of eyesight and technical judgement, it is also a matter of deeper honesty. Judgement has, in a broad sense, a moral dimension, as it requires both a lack of narcissism and a lack of undue modesty; there is a need to both trust and question one's own first impression. To my mind, this adds a fascinating dimension to the game for players and spectators alike.

More generally, the presence of this accurate technology reduces bad feeling between sides, as there are fewer opportunities for accusations of cheating, and for subsequent spirals of retaliation and resentment. Umpires on the whole like the system too, which more often than not proves them right.

The system also includes 'umpire's call', which favours the original decision in marginal cases. It thus retains a degree of precedence for the primary human judgement, allowing for possible minute errors in the equipment. Moreover, this retained element does justice to the difference between what can and what can't be judged by the eye. If for instance a ball turns sharply from outside the line of off stump, it will often be guesswork whether it would have gone on to cut the popping crease by touching the off stump, or whether it would have hit the stump only if it were an inch or two further back. Whereas if the ball swings or spins *along the line* of the stumps (as with the Lyon-to-Stokes ball, bowled round the wicket, pitching on middle and leg, and straightening down the line of the stumps), the umpire should be able to judge by eye with sufficient human certainty that it would have gone on to hit the stumps, and be confident enough to give the batsman out even when the ball has hit the front leg.

Third, the likelihood of being found out (by technology if not by the umpire) makes batsmen more likely to walk when they know they are out. Off the field too, increased surveillance leads to improvement in outward behaviour. (I read that theft in a bicycle parking area was reduced by large-scale depictions of eyes overlooking the space – even the *idea* of being overlooked appears to reduce opportunistic or other crime. This may, of course, be a matter of crime or cheating being relocated rather than reduced).

Some may argue that surveillance leads to a merely surface honesty and reveals trickiness at a deeper level. Once the reviews have been used up, do batsmen revert to old ways – not walking, for example? But even if this does happen at times, good attitudes are also a matter of forming good habits.

And I doubt that human nature changes very much.

Umpires are human. We often think of players' nerves, but umpires too are vulnerable. Several years ago, I was invited to speak at an ICC conference for 'Elite List' international umpires near Cape Town. I spoke about aiming at the truth in both perception and decision-making. The discussion opened up into factors that interfered with this truthfulness, including the umpire's own anxiety.

One umpire present, Daryl Harper, told me how nervous he always was at the start of a big match. Like batsmen and bowlers, he said, umpires have to 'play themselves in', getting used to the bounce and pace of the pitch, as well as to the tense atmosphere. In one test, before DRS was in use, Harper recalled a huge appeal when the second ball of the first over of the match hit the pad. He said: 'I hardly saw it. I had to give it not out.' I thought this was a human admission of a failing that any of us could well imagine. I was reminded of the second ball of the Headingley Test in 1977, bowled by Jeff Thomson. It was well wide of my off stump and I played a terrible stroke to it, hitting the ground (but not the ball) with my bat. I was given out caught behind by umpire Lloyd Budd. Two of us in the same boat.

The celebrated umpire Dickie Bird often showed his anxiety on the field, so much so that I once said to him, gently I think, that whereas he should have been looking after us we had to look after him. I was never sure how much his nerves were part of his act, and how much they were the starting point necessitating his act. I think both, but particularly the latter. (I have learned that when as young men, he and his friend Jack Birkenshaw, another Yorkshire hopeful, who later played for Leicestershire and England, went to variety shows, Dickie was always the first to answer the invitation to come up on stage.)

At every level, when as human beings umpires embody a good spirit, this is likely to be communicated to players. Bird would smile when giving a batsman out run-out, and I always felt it was a smile of pleasure at seeing the truth. I mentioned earlier Marais Erasmus's avuncular authority in quietly shepherding England batsman Jason Roy towards the pavilion when he was wrongly given out and was rooted to the crease.

NurPhoto/Getty Images

Umpires and referees aim to occupy the narrow territory between officiousness and indulgence. In rugby, for instance, games can be spoiled by a referee who fails to let the game flow. Leaving no room either for warnings and friendly guidance, or for giving the benefit of doubt in marginal instances to the possible offender, he blows the whistle for every minute infringement. He gives the impression of relishing his power. He becomes a self-important martinet. And once he has set standards high early in the game, he has to (or feels he has to) live up to them throughout.

A more tactful, more facilitating referee will forcefully shout to players to get back from offside, or near-offside, positions. He will try to avert infringements rather than penalise each one. He will warn scrum halves against putting the ball straight in to their back row, setting an expectation of fair inputs, rather than instantly giving penalties for what is often accepted. He will recognise that it may be impossible for a tackled player to release the ball and roll away instantly, so he will leave some room for proper effort in this regard.

A parallel case in cricket occurs in the calling of no-balls. I don't deny that it is vital to call actual no-balls whenever they occur, both to protect batsmen against unfair deliveries, and to protect bowlers from being called only when they take a wicket but have their moral victory annulled when the legality of the delivery is discovered after the event. But I remember Tony Dodemaide, an Australian Test bowler in the 1980s, telling me that in his day English umpires were helpful to bowlers rather than officious, warning them that they were getting dangerously close to bowling no-balls. These days, this is particularly relevant in international matches, now that each dismissal is checked by the third umpire for no-balls. Indeed, the new procedure raises a possibility of a 'mischief' occurring, namely, that no-balls are allowed to creep in unnoticed, and are only discovered once they have resulted in a batsman being dismissed (or appearing to have been), after the TV umpire has checked. Such events frustrate players and spectators alike. A more proactive, less rigid attitude by the umpires, along the lines Dodemaide refers to, would lessen the chances of this mischief. Indeed, umpires do sometimes act in this communicative way, when they ostentatiously place their own foot just over or touching on the popping crease, and then scratch the crease to make it more easily visible. They may look the bowler in the eye, their shrug indicating that the bowler is pushing his luck and has had his last chance.

Umpires and referees may, of course, err the other way, being too lenient. Then players get the idea that anything goes. Rugby tackles become more dangerous, bowlers come to think that they are entitled to bowl any number of bouncers, against any quality of batsman.

On the large social scale, there are arguments for law-officers confronting, warning or even charging people for minor antisocial offences, like littering public streets, on the grounds that criminality (or cheating) burgeons as a result of letting people get away with small things. But the other side of this coin is that people's lives may thus be ruined by a moment of thoughtlessness or negligence.

Overall, the role of umpires extends far beyond simply making decisions. The umpire's demeanour is important in all this. He has to be generous as well as firm, understanding as well as just. These non-measurable qualities are crucial. And each umpire has to do it his own way.

At best, umpires exercise a containing authority, combining in their demeanour kindness, humour and firmness.

Former umpire Simon Taufel refers to 'man-management and discretion': 'It narrows our view of umpires if we regard the job as all about statistics – about "outs" and "not outs". You don't always need to follow the *strict letter* to achieve your objective. Not all situations are the same, or can be neatly put into one box or other – that's where the skill lies. It's hard to measure, but the "gutometer" knows.'

I remember a droll character called Ron Lay, who had played cricket for Northants, become a policeman, and later umpired in county cricket. He would in a kindly way hand out Polo mints if you found yourself fielding near him at square leg. I once tried to persuade him that a game we were likely to win (at Buxton, against Derbyshire) should not yet be called off because of rain, which was, I had to admit, torrential. He grinned at me. 'There's a difference between farting and tearing your arsehole,' he riposted, and called off the game.

The umpire has to tread another line: that between being aware of well-earned reputations, by teams or individuals, for cynicism or trickery (for example, for footballers who deliberately 'fall' in the penalty area in the hopes of deceiving the referee into awarding a penalty), and on the other hand keeping an open mind, not prejudging. Here it is hard to find the right balance between prejudice (seeing what you expect to see), and naivety (being conned by the cynical).

I'm aware that many of my comments in this section and elsewhere refer to umpiring at high-level professional matches. In most matches, for sure, there will not be DRS. What about the game more generally? There have been reports of increases in the amount of abusive language directed at umpires, especially in the amateur game. There have been calls for the use of yellow or red cards for the sport, calls that so far, I'm glad to say, have been resisted.

I believe attitudes do percolate down; televised and reported cricket gives people some sense of umpiring neutrality, clarity, firmness and basic friendliness.

I think too that, however important DRS has become, and will become, no machinery or technology can replace the human hand and the human heart and eye. Nor can the need for tact and firmness be written into the law. Umpires need all the qualities of a good, human judge or policeman. They cannot be replaced by algorithms or computers.

Finally, one quality in many a top umpire is that people hardly notice his presence. He is neither too prominent nor too absent.

He spots problems before they become incidents, and deals with small incidents before they become big ones. He reads people as well as the game.

* * *

Spirit of cricket applies also to administrators. One element in the sandpaper affair was that within a few months most of the senior employees of the Australian Cricket Board had left, swept away by the brush they had themselves used to banish Smith, Warner and Bancroft. It was sensed, I think, that the players' win-at-all-costs mentality had been encouraged if not inculcated and urged on by the whole system. While the music played, ACB kept dancing, and to its tune.

One feature of Lord's as I experienced it as a young man was an uneasy air of feudalism. I remember a member of the Middlesex Committee coming to the dressing room. He wore a dark pinstripe suit, with a whitish-grey tie. His watch-chain dangled from his pocket. With his pink, closely shaved cheeks and jowly jaw, his perhaps anxiously smug smile, he conveyed an aura of self-importance, though he was doing his best to be friendly. I could imagine what it might have been like for a factory worker during a visitation to the workplace by a boss or a bishop in a scene from Trollope or Dickens.

When I became captain of Middlesex in 1971, a member of the committee mentioned to me, sotto voce: 'Of course you must have a private income.' Well, no, actually. And my income (£1,600 for a six-month contract) was exactly what I had just been paid for twelve months each year as a lecturer at the University of Newcastle-upon-Tyne. This committee man too was well-meaning; but the assumption was that people of his – and, he presumed, my – class needed and deserved more than any mere lecturer (or professional cricketer) to live in the style to which we (he and I) were accustomed and entitled.

Indeed, pay, or rather the paucity of it, was a central factor in the Packer 'revolution' of 1977. It was the main reason players accepted Packer's invitation. Those of us who played in the Centenary Test in March of that year, when the plot was, I learned afterwards, developed, used to joke that we were the worst-paid among all the 250,000 who came to the ground to watch the match (probably not strictly true, but not far off either). The people who ran cricket were not acutely aware of this (to say the least). Their attitude was paternalistic. Cricketers were regarded as wage-earning subordinate employees, not as independent people at the top of their profession or trade, whose skills were in demand and who risked public humiliation if they were unfortunate or careless. Moreover, careers were short and prospects uncertain. Feudalism has its good side. There is a 'benign face of elitism' (as a psychotherapy colleague once described me when I was defending the right of the Institute of Psychoanalysis to a sort of patent on the title 'psychoanalyst'). But the bad side is the implied threat that power bestows. The message to professional cricketers was: 'Be good, show respect to us, be grateful and subtly submissive. Don't forget we can dispense with you at the drop of a hat.'

It was not only a matter of money, then, it's also stereotyping from a position of superiority. Remember Lord Hawke's dictum in 1925: 'Pray God that no professional shall ever captain England. I love and admire them all, but we have always had an amateur skipper, and when the day comes that we shall have no more amateurs captaining England, it will be a thousand pities.'

So it was not only on the basis of race or caste, not only in colonial West Indies or in Hindu India, that this kind of superiority (as in the matter of captaincy) applied; it was closer to home. No wonder Middlesex players ran me out twice in the match when, playing for the Second XI at Hove as a schoolboy in 1960, I was sent upstairs to change with (amateur) captain Charles Robins in a large carpeted drawing room with luxurious though worn armchairs, while the ten professionals were huddled in a box-like room two storeys below. No wonder there were two versions of Mike Atherton's nickname – FEC – on first playing for Lancashire: Future England Captain and Fucking Educated C***.

An example of administrators acting against the spirit of fair play occurred more recently. ICC, which runs international cricket, has now (in 2020) twelve full members, each representing a Test-playing country. Until recently, there were no independent members on the board or the committees. One problem with this set-up was that the primary responsibility of each member was to his (it was always 'his') own board, and his own country. A troubling outcome was that ICC was not running the game overall, disinterestedly, with the interests of all acknowledged and served. It was, rather, a club in which everyone looked after himself, with intimidation from some quarters, appeasement from others. A feature was the power of India to twist arms as a result of its financial clout.

One outcome of this kind of procedure has been the failure to rationalise the timetable of international cricket so as to provide windows for Test cricket.

In 2014, a 'makeover' (or 'takeover') plan emerged after secret negotiations between the representatives of India, England and Australia (the 'Triad', as I called them). This was a scheme to be pushed through ICC, as a result of which these countries were to become both the governors of the international game and the chief beneficiaries of the wealth it produced. The rationale for distributing funds was to be changed in their favour, on the grounds that the sums generated by the three, particularly by India with their vast viewing public, were much higher than those generated by the other boards. Moreover, according to their plan, restrictions were to be brought in that for several years would reserve to the big three (i.e. themselves) key leadership roles in the form of the chairmanship of the main board and the most influential committees. Only thus, they claimed, would efficiency be achieved. And finally, only if the big money-spinning competitions were to be held in these three countries, over the next few years at least, would they be run successfully and profitably. The plan was a way to ensure that India remained solidly within ICC, and to keep them accountable, to England and Australia if to no one else. This was a revolution by the already successful, an anti-democratic coup. No doubt there was a need for more central and powerful governance of the game, but this amounted to a hijack.

Fortunately, the new president of BCCI, appointed for a second time in 2015, was Shashank Manohar, who was elected chair of ICC in the same year. He is still, at the time of writing, in this latter post. Manohar, who had accused his predecessor in both roles, N. Srinivasan, of 'egoistic and autocratic behaviour' that had 'tarnished the reputation of the Board', saw the injustice of this takeover, and has done a good deal to reverse it. He is regarded as a man of integrity.

11

L'ESPRIT DE L'ESCALIER

'No two lions are alike.'

Christopher Flood, lion keeper at
Dublin Zoo, 1900–1933

So far my cricketing examples showing the spirit of cricket (or lack of it) require some knowledge of technicalities. Here I describe admirable character traits, displayed on and off the field, unrelated to the specifics of cricket and its practices.

* * *

During the Third Test in Saint Lucia in 2019, words passed between Shannon Gabriel, the West Indies fast bowler, and Joe Root, England's captain. It transpired that Gabriel said to Root, who was batting: 'Why are you smiling? Do you like boys?' This was not heard publicly but Root's reply was picked up by stump microphones. What he said was: 'Don't use that as an insult. There's nothing wrong with being gay.'

Now, Root's grin can be annoying. Opponents may experience him as laughing at their misfortune. Late in the evening after England had won the 2015 Champions Trophy match at Edgbaston, David Warner allegedly threw a punch at Root for what he experienced as his mocking the Australians, either by smiling provocatively, or by wearing an Australian hat as a wig. As Hamlet says of Claudius, one can smile and smile and be a villain. Not, of course, that Root is a villain, nor that any of this would justify retaliation. My own impression is that his grin is more his way of reassuring himself when he has just survived an error or had some good luck. He looks like the cat with the cream.

In Saint Lucia, his response was immediate and spontaneous. He had had no opportunity to plan. He was civil, calm and matter-of-fact. There was no emphatic self-righteousness, nor any air of retaliation. It seemed like the response of a man comfortable in his sexuality, and non-judgemental about that of others.

There is a French expression, *l'esprit d'escalier*, for thinking of a perfect riposte too late, as described by Denis Diderot: 'The sensitive man – myself for example – wholly focused on someone's criticism, becomes speechless, losing my head in confusion and only regaining it at the bottom of the staircase.'

That is, we often think of what we might have responded (but didn't) just as we've left the scene. We have missed our chance. Root didn't miss his.

Aristotle argued that morality is largely a matter of having established good habits of behaviour, so that doing the right thing happens as a result of our second nature (if not our first). And this is what was so impressive about Root's coolness.

* * *

I like the fact that the French word *esprit* – spirit – appears in the phrase.

This presence of mind reminds me of another international captain, Virat Kohli. What I became aware of first was his impressive intervention at a celebration of cricketing links between India and England over the seven decades of India's independence. I wrote about this in *On Cricket*. Here I will simply say that, at a social party at Lord's, hosted by the Indian High Commissioner, during an interview with one of the old cricketers present, Kohli interrupted to tick off members of the audience who had started to chat loudly among themselves; he asked politely for the microphone, stepped forward and crisply requested respect and attention towards these ex-players. I was impressed. It's one thing to respond to questions (as he himself did later) in an official capacity, when one's authority and duty to speak are clearly established; quite another to interrupt the flow – and indeed the irritating distractions – without invitation. This involved chutzpah, a sense of inbuilt authority and leadership that went beyond the ordinary. Here was a man with an independent mind. Several aspects of his personal charisma, including articulacy and passion, were present for all to see.

I now learn of further such actions by Kohli. One concerned an issue that I have referred to more than once – the jeering at the Australian players involved in the sandpaper debacle when they returned to international cricket in England in 2019. In the World Cup match between India and Australia at the Oval, while Kohli was batting, Smith was booed by Indian fans when fielding on the boundary and greeted with shouts of 'cheater'. Kohli gestured to the fans to applaud him instead, publicly dissociating himself from their attitude.

Kohli was awarded the ICC Spirit of Cricket Award for this gesture. Later he said: 'What happened [i.e. the sandpaper incident] was a long time ago and it is not good to see someone down like that. We have had a few arguments on the field, but you don't want to see a guy feeling like that every time he plays. Because there were so many Indian fans here, I didn't want them to set a bad example. I felt bad because if I was in a position where . . . if I had apologised and done everything asked of me, and was still getting booed, I would not be happy, so I said sorry on behalf of the crowd.' At the award ceremony, Kohli added: 'It was very natural. I never planned [it]. To take advantage of someone's emotion wasn't correct. I just stood up for that. It wasn't to gain anything out of it.'

Once again, Kohli went beyond the call of duty. He put his head above the parapet, he 'stood up for' something important, publicly going against a prevalent view, challenging a powerful group. The action on the field was more important than the words he later used. Like Root, he seized the moment, doing so spontaneously.

I have another story about Kohli, told to me by Suresh Menon, editor of the now defunct *Wisden India*. The two men were having breakfast together at the team hotel in Chennai, before a test match. Kohli was to be named 'Cricketer of the Year' in the publication, and the editor had arranged a conversation before writing the piece. A crowd collected, wanting selfies, autographs – the usual. As the group grew, Kohli addressed them: 'I am having breakfast with this gentleman, it would be bad manners to break away. I assure you that once we are done, I shall oblige each one of you.' Having mollified the group, he sat down and told Menon: 'You know, sir, some of these fans come from great distances. I hate to disappoint them. I might be the only cricketer they ever meet.'

As Suresh said, this was old-fashioned good manners allied with a keen awareness of a sportsman's responsibility to his fans. And he spoke out both personally and publicly.

He has also been willing to act as a representative – of 'the people and the nation'. His remarks to Menon remind me of Sachin Tendulkar's response when I congratulated him on taking time out to offer *namaste* to a groundswoman in a red sari at the end of the Chennai Test match following the terrorist atrocities in Mumbai: 'We don't play for ourselves. We play for India. Thanks to God, I have been able to play for India for twenty years. It is wonderful for the nation to have a victory in such a fine match.'

On receiving the award, Kohli said (of the booing and derision for Smith), 'It is a representation of who we are as people, of who we are as a nation.'

Here is one further example of willingness to stand up, this time not from a cricketer, but from the historian, Ramachandra Guha, who wrote the magisterial biography of Gandhi. In December 2019, the Indian government published their new citizenship law, making those who had suffered 'religious persecution in their country of origin eligible for Indian citizenship' – *unless they were Muslims.* This outrageous exception, along with other anti-Muslim policies and statements, led to protests. One peaceful protester was Guha. He was speaking about Gandhian ideas of pluralism when he was summarily arrested and detained for five hours. In joining the protest, Guha too seized the moment. He didn't wait, or say he had other engagements. And he represented not only himself, but the man he had written about, Gandhi, one of whose four main self-sacrificing campaigns had been for Hindu–Muslim rapprochement. Gandhi was, don't forget, murdered by a member of the nationalist RSS, an extreme but significant element of which is still active now in the government's BJP party. Gandhi's crime, in the eyes of RSS, was that he was a traitor to the fundamentalist Hindu cause.

To return to Kohli. On the field as well as off it his presence is palpable. As was the case with Viv Richards, it's hard not to look at him; he draws one's attention. He's keen, lean, dynamic, totally involved. Watch Kohli and you sense from his reactions a great deal about the way the game is going. He wears his emotions on his sleeve. Along with passionate desire and high standards, he expresses communal team reactions, the pleasure of joint success and the desolation of shared disappointment. If he believes the opposition have behaved badly, he will speak his mind bluntly, on the field there and then.

As a leader Kohli is aggressive, sometimes brash. Tactically, he's shrewd and inventive, always looking for opportunities to attack. He lives by, and expects from his team, a strong work ethic. He also demands attention to detail. As a batsman, he regularly turns singles into twos, especially when chasing a target. Less athletic partners may be run off their feet. I suspect he has little patience with laziness.

His run-hunger is apparent. He is hawk-eyed, quick-witted, quick-footed, all energy. His conversion rate in turning 50s into 100s (53.8 per cent not long ago) has been second only to Bradman's (69 per cent). (Root's has been 25 per cent.) He has stamina, drive and persistence. Taking account of all three formats, he's clearly the most versatile batsman in the world, averaging over 50 in each.

Noting his extraordinary ability to make use of the classical alongside the innovative even in the shortest forms of the game, Menon wrote: 'His understanding of space and time is unrivalled.' He's truly an Einstein among batsmen.

Root's remark in Trinidad and Kohli's behaviour in several contexts both exemplify the fact that there are no rules for this kind of courage. Cricket – a series of contests between two protagonists in the context of the team – reveals character, whether we like it or not. Situations crop up out of the blue, without previous scripting.

And that's one element in the appeal of cricket (perhaps, in its slower pace and longer timespan, even more so than of other sports). It may be a quality that one may develop through cricket, though this would be hard to establish.

More generally, moral qualities hang together, they are inter-dependent; courage requires judgement or temperance if it is not to become bravado; patience requires a willingness to act if not to subside into stolidity and passivity. Even in pragmatic terms, qual-ities are not isolated; you need much more than technical skill to be a good batsman, bowler, captain or coach. You need also resil-ience, a willingness to learn, a hunger to improve and the good sense to discriminate between advice that suits you and advice that will militate against your own strengths and those of the team. And much more.

Playing cricket well calls for many personal qualities – for patience and restraint, for emotion and spontaneity. No two situations are precisely alike, which means that the quality of courage is not only habitual (which Aristotle stressed), it is also creative, calling for unique, off-the-cuff responses to each unique situation. Root and Kohli exemplify both. In cricket, and especially given the tempo of the traditional game, we need to have room for both innovation *and* orthodoxy, for common sense *and* the overriding of common sense. We need checks and balances, internally and externally.

* * *

When Mr Flood the lion keeper at Dublin Zoo was asked the secret for never having lost a lion cub in long years of work, he said: 'No two lions are alike'. Therefore looking after lions in a zoo is not just a matter of applying rules. And yet of course they are all lions, and lions do what lions do. Every baby is also unique. But with babies too: babies do what babies do.

I was once asked if I might write a book on the science of captaincy – I would be reluctant to do so. As with Mr Flood and his lions, I see the exciting aspects of captaincy more as a matter of responding freshly to each situation than of being habituated in good practice (though both are mandatory). There are (of course) general rules for captaincy as for individual cricketing skills, and it's true that often the best way is to follow well-trodden paths of common sense and good technique. But it's more of an art than a science.

For captains such creativity is required even more than for other members of the team. Shane Warne's prediction before the 2019 World Cup that the best-led team would win it expresses the key importance of this ingredient. And though I don't know who the best captain was, Eoin Morgan is undoubtedly a very good one.

12

HOMO LUDENS

'Cricket will become a boys' game again, for an occasional
afternoon . . . a grown man may feel the urge from time to
time to smite the ball or to bring off some stupendous running
catch . . . Yet it may in the end be for the good: it is good that
nations grow up. It is good that they cease from childish things.'

Rowland Bowen

What I have written so far about the spirit of cricket has been mainly
at the level of fair play as opposed to cheating and trickery. I have also
suggested that the spirit of the game goes beyond the Laws. Here I
want to broaden the range of values that cricket (and other sports)
brings to life. I will suggest that at best cricket expresses and invites a
deeper set of value-laden attitudes. It offers a larger scope for personal
development. Sport may be the locus of personal growth. It is largely
through play that this occurs.

Here is psychoanalyst Wilfred Bion, writing about his schooldays:

When I reached the Main School, I had become proficient at
games. Games were in themselves enjoyable; I was fortunate not
to have had them buried under a mass of subsidiary irrelevancies
such as winning matches, keeping my ghastly sexual impulses
from obtruding, and preserving a fit body for the habitation of

a supposedly healthy mind. I liked swimming; I enjoyed water polo; I could be indifferent to the rivalry with others for a place in the team. I was equally fortunate in rugger. It was soon obvious that I was good; I was first-class at every game but cricket – at which I was so bad that it presented no problem. I could, therefore, come nearer to playing the game for the sake of the game than I ever came to working for the sake of work.

Interestingly, he went on to tell how his 'excellence meant that the prospects of captainship began to appear over the horizon. That would mean that games for the sake of games would no longer be a feasible aim.'

I presume Bion meant that if he were to captain a side he would have to accommodate further purposes, of looking to the well-being and interrelationships of the players and of concentrating on tactics, and all this would intrude on playing for its own sake. Play would have become work.

Sport may also be a locus of prejudice and narrow-mindedness. As Ranjitsinhji memorably wrote (in 1897): 'Some players grow grey in the service of the game and learn nothing.' And Alan Knott, England's wicketkeeper, once said to me that he knew professional cricketers who had been in the game for fifteen years and had failed to develop either as players or as people.

Here are some ways in which cricket may enhance personal growth.

* * *

In 1938 the Dutch historian Johan Huizinga wrote his classic book on play and civilisation, *Homo Ludens*. He argued that play pre-dates civilisation and underlies it. Its basic ingredients are to be found in animals (and young human animals, i.e. children). Watch puppies or lion cubs playing, he suggests, and you have the essential features.

First, there is spontaneous mutual activity, set apart from the business of survival or making a living; activity that is not directly pragmatic. Second, there are rules – don't bite, or not too hard. Third, there is a sort of 'ceremoniousness'. Fourth, they pretend to get angry. And fifth, there is evident pleasure in their 'merry gambols'.

For Huizinga, play is essentially childlike. It is self-generating and serves no further purpose other than the activity itself. It is not solemn though it is often serious. It is all-absorbing. It has built-in limits, particularly on aggression.

Theorists, he continues, try to establish a biological function for play; but this is a mistake, for it takes attention away from the nature of play itself. There is no reason for playing beyond the thing itself.

> The intensity of, and absorption in, play finds no explanation in biological analysis. Yet in this intensity, this absorption, this maddening, lies the very essence and primordial quality of playing.

Bion's remarks echo this idea of a primordial notion of play. Another psychoanalyst, Marion Milner, writes in a similar vein about the states of utter concentration, absorption and ecstasy that feature both in play and in art. She speaks of the temporary loss of the self, of the fire of concentration, the melting down of the old, sometimes precociously developed, separate self. She writes of transcendence; in the child's world, toys are transformed, as are furniture and spaces – my granddaughter once said of the room where she and I played that when I wasn't there it was no longer, magically, '[the] beach', it was 'only a room with two sofas' (as she put it in sad tones over the phone). In such states of absorption sharp boundaries, both between things in the world and between self and other, are also temporarily transcended; the child, and the child in the artist, temporarily *become* the thing they are painting. My granddaughter again: she was given a toy dog as a take-home present at a party. When she made dog noises in the back of the car, I asked her if she was talking to it in dog language. 'No, Mike,' she said scornfully, 'I'm *being* the dog. Don't you know that's what toys are for?' Play may involve imagination – becoming someone or something else.

For Huizinga too, if play takes on ulterior motives or aims it ceases to be 'the game for the sake of the game'. One corollary, he argues, is that organised games or sports run the risk of becoming sterile, having lost their essential features. There is too much emphasis on winning, and therefore on discipline and rules. In today's world, he would see intensive practice, computer analysis and rigorous train-ing as wearing away playfulness. Joe Root hinted at this risk, when he said in an interview that too much information gets in the way of spontaneity. For Huizinga, professional sport becomes a matter of relentless and over-serious pragmatism. Sport becomes a business.

> The great ball-games in particular require the existence of per-manent teams, and herein lies the starting-point of modern sport . . . Ever since the last quarter of the nineteenth century games, in the guise of sport, have been taken more and more

seriously. The rules have become increasingly strict and elaborate. Records are established at a higher, or faster, or longer level
than was ever conceivable before. Everybody knows the delightful
prints from the first half of the nineteenth century, showing cricketers in top-hats . . . . Now, with the increasing systematization
and regimentation of sport, something of the pure play-quality is
inevitably lost. We see this very clearly in the official distinction
between amateurs and professionals (or 'gentlemen and players' as
used pointedly to be said). It means that the play-group marks out
those for whom playing is no longer play, ranking them inferior to
the true players in standing but superior in capacity.

The spirit of the professional is no longer the true play-spirit; it stops
being carefree; regimentation displaces love – as in the amatory root
of 'amateur'.

Topical Press Agency/Stringer/Getty Images

(At this point the translator of the 1950 edition – Huizinga himself
had died in 1945 – adds two footnotes, enlarging on this theme.
First, he comments that: 'Our author may not have been sufficiently

familiar with the development of "sport" in the last ten or twenty years . . . to stress the all-important point that sport has become a business, or, to put it bluntly, a commercial racket.' The second note is a quotation from G. K. Chesterton: "'If a thing is worth doing at all, it is worth doing badly.'")

A few lines later, Huizinga continues: 'The fatal shift to over-seriousness has also infected the non-athletic games where calculation is everything.'

In short, though organised sport (and particularly professional sport) retains elements of what he considers to be the essence of play – the hallowed space set apart, the rules of the game along with an aspiration to the spirit of fair play – he believes that the activity skews away from other essentials, particularly in the degree of planning, organisation and practice. Being paid to play adds, according to him, another dimension that goes against the child-aspects; it increases the risk of the game losing its sense of fun (so central to animals and small children wrestling and playing).

Cricket writer Rowland Bowen has a similarly dyspeptic view of pro-fessional sport, specifically with regard to what he thought had become of cricket after the Second World War. Writing in 1970, he states:

> The theme of this book [a history of cricket] is of rise, life and decline . . . The basic trouble . . . may be summed up in one word as over-professionalism . . . If people who think of cricket as a holy game had not been so conscious of their own impor-tance [and had realised] that cricket is just a game and not an ethic, then something might have been done.

Cricket will survive, he thinks, but:

> [It] will become a boy's game again, for an occasional after-noon . . . a grown man may feel the urge from time to time to smite

the ball or to bring off some stupendous running catch . . . Yet it may in the end be for the good: it is good that nations grow up. It is good that they cease from childish things.

His views are, I think, discordant with each other. On the one hand he celebrates and revels in boyish spontaneity. On the other we should give up childish things. He predicts that by the end of the twentieth century cricket would still be found, but only 'played for pleasure'. But then he says: 'This is no trough into which the game has fallen: it is a decline into the grave.'

'Really to play, a man must play like a child,' Huizinga writes. And Bowen agrees.

So what do I make of this critique?

In my view, both in their different ways are right to say that there are risks of 'over-professionalism', but wrong to say that this factor takes away the 'play' element. I think they are mistaken both in logic and in relation to matters of fact and experience.

First, logic. The philosopher Ludwig Wittgenstein used the concept of 'family resemblances' to illustrate how we use terms in language and thinking; how it is that different particular instances fall under general concepts. The example he gives is, interestingly, games. He suggests that instead of insisting on necessary and sufficient conditions that can or should be laid down for such a concept as 'game' there are 'family resemblances' – networks of similarities and overlaps – between, say, card-games and ball-games, between skipping with a rope and playing mummies and daddies, between gambling and games that involve strength and skill. As there also are, I would add, between one game and another within each category. As Wittgenstein says:

I can think of no better expression to characterise these similar-ities than 'family resemblances'; for the various resemblances between members of a family: build, features, colour of eyes, gait, temperament, etc. etc. overlap and criss-cross in the same way. – And I shall say: 'games' form a family . . . The kinds of number form a family in the same way. Why do we call something a 'number'? Well, perhaps because it has a direct relationship with several things that have hitherto been called number; and this can be said to give it an indirect relationship to other things we call the same name. And we extend our concept of number as in spinning a thread we twist fibre on fibre. And the strength of the thread does not reside in the fact that some one fibre runs through its whole length, but in the overlapping of many fibres.

Thus, the Huizinga play-concept is one such strand, a central and important one, but not sufficient or even necessary for a game to be a game. An activity may become less playful, but still a game. We may indeed lose touch with this strand. We may fall into a depleted sense of play (as described by Brendon McCullum) in which love and attention have drained away. We may even, paradoxically, be inclined to ask in the whole of sport is there a real game? The spirit of play, like the spirit of Christmas in Dickens's Mr Scrooge, may be overlaid and distorted by cynicism and reductionism. Huizinga is offering a persuasive re-definition, pushed towards a paradox.

Second, as to facts of experience. Though the joy *may* go out of the playing of the game, though bitterness and burn-out may creep in, in my experience this is not happening in professional cricket, nor has it happened in any general way. Being paid does not mean that playing for enjoyment disappears. The love impulse is not at all restricted to the non-paid, the 'amateurs'. As McCullum said, we cricketers have to remind ourselves from time to time why we played the game as children, why we were drawn into it in the first place – for love of the game. But we should not suppose that this love impulse is bound to be dissipated. It isn't. We still get a thrill from taking a 'stupendous running catch'. We can at times trust our bodies; we have to, in the moment of action. As Milner wrote of playing table tennis: 'What surprised me was that my arm seemed to know what to do by itself, it was able to make the right judgements of strength and direction quite without my help.'

In my view, the playing of sport as a grown-up involves *retaining the child, while accommodating the adult* – itself not a bad rough or preliminary definition of development. When a small child dances uninhibitedly, she enters into the dance with her whole body. As we grow older, it is hard to retain the capacity to act from our whole selves, to undo sharp boundaries achieved by cleverness and a sometimes mis-applied rationality. Looking and seeing in an absorbed way is necessary if we are not to see the world as alien, sterile and dull.

There are, for children and adults, two possible dangers. One is to be stuck in an imaginary world, in an illusion or delusion as in a dream or nightmare; which is to risk madness. A patient told me once about medieval ballads in which children are stolen away in the night by evil fairies, and never return – an image of her own fear of a permanent loss of sanity. At the other extreme lies the meaningless state of depression or a sense of pointlessness, in which, in Wordsworth's haunting words, 'getting and spending we lay waste our powers'.

At its best, sport, even top-level professional sport, involves an oscillation between conscious control, with a narrow, even quasi-scientific focus, a left-brain way of functioning, and another, broader, right-brain kind of approach. Having at first played like Bowen's boy or Huizinga's child, we have, sometimes explicitly and consciously, to learn discipline. We have to practise and groove our actions. We need to review our strengths and weaknesses. We helpfully keep an observing eye on our moment-to-moment shifts in concentration, focus and technique. We need both modes of attention.

Love of the game allows us not only to struggle through, working at our technique and fitness even when we are reluctant to do so, but also to let go of earnestness and over-thinking. As in love between people, we have to work at both. We have to struggle through the difficulties and tensions, but also relinquish at times argument and complaint. We need to sustain conscious effort but also be willing to let go.

Playing cricket, once we are out in the middle, bowling or batting, we have to trust ourselves, our training, our eyes and our bodies. We need background ideas about how to approach different situations or challenges, or what to look for from certain bowlers, or where we might score a boundary against them. We may set ourselves to let go of anything outside the line of our eyes, anything safely outside the off stump – think of Steve Smith or Virat Kohli batting against Jimmy Anderson. Yet from within such frames of mind, we have to trust ourselves to respond to each ball appropriately. We may look either more narrowly, or less, at what our antagonist is doing. Watching the bowler run up, we may attend to the explicit, focused question – one example would be: on which side does he have the shiny half of the ball? Alternatively, we may also allow ourselves to attend more broadly to the overall impression of the bowler in his run-up and action, trusting ourselves to gauge subliminally which way the ball is likely to swing or simply to respond to whatever happens.

We need to allow room to surprise ourselves with a spontaneous response; but we may also need to maintain our patient resolve to let the ball go, unless we see a half volley or a short ball, which we can pounce on and hit for four through the off side, à la Smith or Kohli.

I know that my shortcomings as a batsman were a mixture of failings of both kinds. I did not allow myself to become fully and explicitly enough aware of bad technical tendencies that crept in from time to time, and which needed specific attention and re-installing. But I also suffered from being too tense. The tension, embodied in holding the bat too tightly, was a result both of anxiety (was I capable of playing at this level?) and of an idea that holding the bat more loosely would produce simply that – looseness.

If a perceptive coach had known me well, and if I had listened to what he might have said or shown me, I would have needed to work at both elements – at both technique and emotion; both on my basic technique with its underlying, partly conscious theories and on my too easily rattled confidence. I needed to be more of a child in order to be more of an adult, more of an adult to be more of a (playful) child.

In this sort of way, sport reflects and amplifies ordinary life. In cricket, in other sports and in the whole of life we need both. We need the capacity to oscillate. We need to trust ourselves to go for it, to get things done, to spread our wings. We need to question ourselves, monitoring ourselves, checking and reflecting on our spontaneity. We should not simply follow our 'instincts', but nor should we ignore or lose touch with them.

* * *

In a blurb for a novel by Elizabeth Strout, Hilary Mantel writes: 'I am deeply impressed. Writing of this quality comes from a commitment to listening, from a perfect attunement to the human condition, from an attention to reality so exact that it *goes beyond a skill and becomes a virtue* [my italics].'

Aristotle for one would have agreed with Mantel; the *arete*, the excellence, best essence or virtue of a person, was in his view living up to his or her potential – the flute player qua flute player, etc., and the human being qua someone living according to reason and to harmony of the soul. Gaining this 'arete' requires proper attention, of both kinds.

Another writer who links skill with virtue via attention is Iris Murdoch, when in *The Sovereignty of Good* she describes learning as central to the good life; it requires a willingness to recognise that the world does not fit in with our own wishes. We have to develop a discipline. In order to learn, we have to have Mantel's commitment to listening and looking, to developing an openness to what is real, a capacity for sustained attention to the world as it actually is. We cannot rely on wishful thinking. Learning a foreign language, Murdoch reminds us, requires a recognition that there is much that we don't know. It calls for disciplined attention; the verbs do not always conjugate regularly – we simply have to memorise them. There is no way around – we have to go through. And proper attention, along with the discipline and humility that enable it, are (broadly) moral qualities.

Skill also means being able to respond to different difficulties, and gradually grow a degree of more or less justified confidence about finding solutions. I once heard a Japanese chief executive say, with disarming simplicity 'I like problems because they give a chance of solutions' – an orientation that tolerates difficulty and struggle.

So the commitment to reality requires a willingness to bear uncertainty, and to keep at it. Works of art, especially innovative ones, make us think outside our boxes, challenging us. I recall an episode of the radio programme *Private Passions* in which Richard Flanagan, author of the novel *The Narrow Road to the Deep North*, chose at least one piece of music he wasn't sure he liked. Questioned on this by the presenter, he replied that he wanted to listen to the piece, live with it, and eventually come to a view. He valued having to deal with the problems of uncertainty and ambivalence, even confusion (in himself), and the difficulties presented by the music. Rivers, he might have added, have rapids as well as gentle smoothness. So, gaining skills, appreciation and understanding requires a willingness to go through a process that doesn't simply feed our narcissism and doesn't always offer instant gratification. Flanagan believes that one of the values and functions of art is to unsettle us, to arouse new, mixed feelings. On his desert island, he would have time to reflect on his mixed feelings about this choice.

This feature – that still becomes virtue – applies in cricket, in sport and in many areas of life.

If so, does lack of skill become vice (or shortcoming, symptom or sin, whatever might be the opposite of virtue)? I think so, at least in some cases.

Here is a small example. In our family, as is common, there is a much greater facility with computers among younger members than among the old. One ordinary result is that I need help when confronted with difficulties. However, this situation tempts me towards panic, anger or impatience as soon as a difficulty arises. I become instantly helpless, and burden people unnecessarily. We tend to become unrealistic in the direction either of never admitting our need for help (we feel humiliated at having to ask), or of becoming pathetic and lacking in self-sufficiency. These attitudes and situations spiral downhill, just as more positive responses spiral upwards.

Lack of skill *is* often carelessness, or an inability to see what we don't want to see, or a result of projection of stuff we can't own on to others, as in stereotyping. As a cricketer I might in my mind convert a good bowler into an unplayable bowler, turning myself into a weakling – or a tensely controlled and limited player – in the process. And then this becomes a reality in the world: I actually become weaker than I am, less resourceful. Or on the other side I turn an ordinarily good bowler into a bad one, thus underestimating him and getting myself out.

We constantly and in all sorts of ways impair our skills. We are out of harmony with ourselves.

At best, however, playfulness both requires and contributes to the freedom to be oneself. Spontaneity and authenticity are important features, as Huizinga emphasised. Playfulness involves, too, the possibility of expansion of the self. I surprise myself. I use more of myself than I am familiar with at other times. Having given myself permission to play, what I come up with feels like a gift, not something willed by me. I feel freer than usual, and therefore open to being more fluent in thought and action. I am less hedged in by fear of disapproval, less inhibited, but on these lovely, rare occasions, neither licentious nor loose. I feel creative. My watchful conscious ego stands back a little, without going absent altogether. It trusts these less conscious aspects. I am, internally, all of a piece, in, not out of, harmony. My work or play becomes less laboured. It even feels easier, more natural, than usual.

We used to call Mike Hendrick, the Derbyshire and England medium-fast bowler, the 'caresser', as he was so relaxed in his action and delivery, holding the ball lightly in his fingertips, not gripping or clutching it tensely. His wrist was loose, adding momentum to the ball as he released it. We often said that he was quicker than he looked. He rarely seemed to be straining. 'Caressing' is a term more often applied to batsmen, for instance, to David Gower when he stroked the ball through the covers without flourish or bludgeon. His timing and grace combined to create unexpected momentum. As with Hendrick, his play often seemed effortless.

I want to make two points here. The first is that, with this kind of relaxed concentration when actions look more like play than work, a broader self is involved than the worrying, anxious and dutiful ego often acknowledges. This state in a single person parallels team spirit within the team. When team spirit is strong, everyone functions at a level beyond individual striving. At such times each person respects the others in the team. Similarly, when play-spirit is strong in the self, the person functions at a higher and more cohesive level. Perhaps this is part of what novelist Albert Camus meant by his remark that he learnt all he knew about the moral interactions of men from playing football. Presumably it was through football that he came to respect others in the team and himself; perhaps within himself too he learned to achieve a higher level of integration.

The second point is that lack of constraint is central to play. Not that there are no limits – puppies bite each other but not too hard. But play implies going beyond a fixed script. The playful person does not know where (s)he will end up. 'Playing with an idea' has a different penumbra of meaning from 'working on an idea'. The former suggests free-ranging experiment with an unknown destination; the latter hints at testing of a more organised kind, an attempt to work out whether a known end will be achieved. I'm not saying that there is always a sharp distinction between them; our best work has strong elements of play, and play is a serious matter.

This leads me to a further point. Common sense (that not-so-common quality) – an important element in work-ethic – is both valuable and limiting. It is not arcane or fancy. It does not require specialist knowledge, though one may need to be experienced in any field to have much chance of embracing and understanding what counts as good sense within that field. Common sense refers to a capacity to see something for what it is. It is down-to-earth, requiring feet to be on the ground. It is a matter of good sense or judgement. A person who has this quality is not erratic or extremist, nor a fanatic. (S)he will pick out of a complex situation what is crucial, and offer a practical assessment or solution, expressing values broadly shared by the community. Yet, on the other hand, common sense is often turned to as a short-cut; it becomes lazy and loses its perspicacity. And in tomorrow's view today's common sense is discredited or *passé*. It can block creativity with its conservatism. It tends to prevent people looking outside the box.

I have argued that laws, of the land as of cricket, are ultimately based on common sense ideas of fairness and balance; they require consideration of the interests of all. It is not for nothing that the symbol of the Central Criminal Court is a pair of scales. The aim is to weigh up the evidence and to come as near common sense as the law makes possible.

I have also said that the law cannot sit still; it needs revision and revaluation in the light of new technologies and evolving attitudes. Moreover, systems of law cannot cover every situation thrown up by chance and change. Nor should law concern itself over-much with inner states that are central to the moral or spiritual life. Nevertheless, there are questions that require us to go beyond the letter of the law, to consult as reflectively as possible our emotional response to various scenarios, including challenges to our sense of the spirit of the game.

Common sense is vital – we need sheriffs to ride out and catch the criminal; we need ordinary justice, with many of its everyday assumptions, and broad tariffs for crimes or for going against the spirit of the game. We need to go along with ordinary notions of responsibility and guilt. However, Jonathan Lear and Donald Moss, both American psychoanalysts, make the point that common sense only takes us so far, and sometimes insists on what turns out later to be false or morally wrong.

Common sense, important as it is, is bound to leave much out. A fuller morality goes beyond the law, into areas that the law cannot and should not enter. Socrates was both a courageous soldier (in practical life) and a questioner of the concept of courage (in personal and philosophical reflection). As a philosopher, he challenged common sense, asking: 'Among all courageous people is there a truly courageous person?' or 'Among all wise people is anyone really wise?' Socratic 'irony' was a matter of questioning the obvious, arousing and giving mental space to uncertainty.

Sometimes the demand for new thinking emerges from painful disruptions in our lives, when our worlds are turned upside down. Occasionally, the disruption gives rise to a creative new conception, either philosophical or personal. Crises of one kind and another may generate transformation, not only at the level of Socrates, but also in everyday growing up and life, in a deepening of our understanding of value and truth. (Crises and traumas may also, by contrast, have negative consequences, producing breakdown. To forestall anxiety, we turn to the gratifications of power and even cruelty, or regress to old certainties.)

I owe some of this thinking to Lear. Similarly, Moss has reminded me that psychoanalysis is not only a continuation of ordinarily sensitive thinking, but a radical questioning of it. Freud re-cast our thinking about thinking through a new lens or frame. He made central to our psychology the idea of our not knowing what goes on in our own minds. He brought to light the presence of dynamic forces within that deny or distort our actual attitudes and thoughts. He showed us how much of our everyday sense of who we are derives from such deformations. Through these distorting frames or glasses we may discover we have often for long periods of time made ourselves a sort of home (or perhaps a retreat, even a prison), in which we already know what is the case without having to attend properly to new phenomena and find new ways to think. Such retreats from reality are means by which we attempt to protect ourselves from the nausea of breakdown or traumatic disruption. We are often relieved to regain this 'common' ground of old safe certainties.

Moss offers as an example one contemporary *aporia* (Socrates's term for being bewildered or at a loss) that we find ourselves in. We are likely to be confused about sexual identities. What had, Moss writes, served us well over generations – that we are born into a gender that our body dictates, and that there are clear standards for normality and deviation – all these have been thrown up in the air by radical ideas about gender identity. A new generation believes that the subjective, declarative 'I' is the (only) gauge, that this 'I' can construct and/or know that I am, for example, really a girl or a woman, not, as previously dictated to me by my body and by society, a boy or a man. Or that I am neither or both. From this new viewpoint, the old certainties are rigid and oppressive, based on fear. Whereas from the point of view of the 'traditionalists' (or 'old fogeys') the trans-lobby is dangerous, ideological or even fundamentalist in its championing of the new, post-modern position. As Moss says, we have, as psychoanalysts and also as ordinary puzzled members of society, to give mental space to both viewpoints.

You may ask: 'But what does this have to do with cricket, and its spirit and Laws?'

Sport presents us with disruption that calls for creative solutions, some new.

When in a state match at Sydney in 2014 Phillip Hughes died as a result of being hit by a bouncer on the back of his neck, the Australian Board's doctor, Peter Brukner, was at pains to reassure us all that this was a freak accident, a one-in-a-billion chance. He wanted to head off a mass panic or withdrawal from playing cricket, or from letting one's children play the game.

Five years on, in August 2019, when Steve Smith lay still on the ground at Lord's, there was panic and fear. Fortunately, he was able to walk off. As there were no apparent short-term problems of concussion, he was also allowed to resume his innings, which he did with courage. Next day, when he woke feeling 'woozy and unclear', he was not allowed to bat. He was not considered for the next Test match – another correct decision.

Writing about injuries to the head just after these last events, Mike Atherton made two important points. He informed us first that the day after the Hughes tragedy, in a Test match in Karachi, the New Zealand team agreed as a mark of respect not to bowl bouncers and not to put a fielder in the dangerous position of short square leg. And second, he pointed out that there had been far more cricket-injury deaths than we (or many of us, including me) knew, most of them at school level or in recreation games far away from the public glare of the professional game. *Wisden Cricketers' Almanack* calculated that between 1850 and 1950 there had been in England alone at least three hundred and fifty cricket-related deaths.

Atherton and I, like almost all professional cricketers, agree that the bouncer is an integral part of cricket, and that it produces, at times, thrilling challenges and spectacles. Fast bowling, as the old Yorkshire batsman Maurice Leyland said, 'keeps you honest'. Nevertheless, I agree with Atherton that we are right to be more cautious about concussion now that more is known about its delayed and potential long-term effects. We are right to insist on helmets being worn by children when playing with a hard ball, and against fast bowling. But risk cannot be ruled out. The challenges that constitute the game include not only technical ones – we can be bamboozled by leg-spin bowlers, like Abdul Qadir or Shane Warne – but also physical – we can be hit on the head or in the ribs by a hard ball travelling at ninety-odd miles an hour from a Jofra Archer or a Dennis Lillee.

In 1976, at the suggestion of Tony Greig (then captain of England), he and I (about to play in my first Test match) arranged to have head-protectors made for us in Nottingham. Greig, who had watched the West Indies fast bowlers in Australia the winter before, and played against Australia's Lillee and Jeff Thomson the season before that, was convinced that sooner or later there were bound to be serious injuries to batsmen. As far as I know, he never used his, but I did mine, the following summer, in five Tests against Australia.

Our innovation was not dramatic or deeply thought out. But it did go against many contemporary ideas of what was appropriate. It went against cricket's common sense. I was well aware of how it might be – and in fact was in some quarters – ridiculed by macho elements in the cricketing world. I was surprised when Rodney Marsh said to me at the end of the 1977 series that he and others completely agreed with the idea of head-protection, they just thought it had to be more comprehensive than mine. Within a year, almost every first-class batsman was wearing a helmet, as were those fielding at short square leg. These helmets were much more substantial than my little plastic skullcap with guards for the temples. The introduction of helmets went against what had been, in many quarters, cricketing common sense.

Other innovations, both by batsmen and bowlers, many of them arrived at for the particular challenges of limited-overs, and in particular T20, cricket, produced similar reactions of incredulity. All require thinking outside the box, defying expectations, risking mockery.

I have been struck by some of the field-placing in recent limited-overs games. During the World Cup in 2019, for instance, the fields regularly set for leg-spinners bore no resemblance to any field set before. Allowed a maximum of five boundary fielders, they tended to have a leg-side field comprising short fine leg, deep square leg, deep mid-wicket and long on. On the off side they would routinely have a long off, an orthodox extra cover, a deep cover point, and two short third men. Thus three of the four fielders required within the circle were behind square. This would have been an inconceivable field-setting in earlier times. Part of its rationale lies in the acceptance by the fielding side, for periods of time, of five, sometimes of six runs an over (the batsmen seeking perhaps seven or eight); another part lies in the greater striking power of batsmen and their bats, hence the need to have fielders on the boundary in front of the batsman in order to catch mishits as well as well-struck shots. With those field placings, captains and bowlers had gone against the everyday assumptions of their earlier selves and of the entire history of cricket. Common sense had been overthrown.

Here is an example of a thought-experiment of mine that in the end went nowhere, though its motivation was to rebalance the game. As chair of the World Cricket Committee, I became aware of changes in patterns of results in Test cricket. One was the inexorable increase in the percentage of series wins by the home side. I felt that this was not a good thing; cricket at its best needs the unpredictable, and this seemed to go against that ideal. Reasons for the trend were manifold – shorter tours meant that visiting teams were not fully acclimatised when the Test matches started, condensing the Test matches into short periods meant that players in those teams had little or no chance of match practice to prove, or improve, their form; and the crowding of the calendar with high-paying domestic T20 leagues across the world meant that some top players were making themselves unavailable for Test match tours. I felt too that there was an additional factor, to do with the preparation of pitches to suit home sides, often encouraged or demanded by home teams and their coaches, managers or boards. I wondered how to counter this trend.

One possible way was to remove the requirement of a toss, and give the choice of innings to the visiting team. That, though, might lead to duller cricket via the preparation of 'safer' pitches (i.e. pitches on which batting would be easy at all stages), or it might unduly favour the visitors. Some suggested having a toss for the First Test, and alternating in subsequent ones. But the trouble with this would be that everyone would then know which pitches might be doctored to favour the home team, and which could be left more neutral.

My somewhat bizarre idea was that at each test there could be a preliminary toss to decide whether there would be a toss. For those matches randomly allotted no toss, the visitors would get choice of innings. Thus no one could know in advance which side would have the choice: often crucial if the pitches are either grassy and damp at the start – so one would want to bowl first – or dry and liable to turn more and more – so everyone would want to bat first. The overall outcome of my plan would be that the home side would have the choice in 25 per cent of matches, the other 75 per cent going to the away team. But no one would know in advance which matches would be which, or whether these statistics would apply in any particular series.

This idea did not find favour. I think it was too complicated and too difficult to make intelligible to cricket supporters in general. Cricket is already in some ways arcane: lbw laws for example are, necessarily in my view, complicated; the mechanics of swing bowling are obscure to almost everyone, including it seems to physicists or engineers familiar with air pressure and swerve. My idea was over-intellectual and doomed to failure. But that does not mean that it was a bad thing to think of it and give it an airing.

Willingness to question common sense requires recognition that not every new whim is justified. It's not right that anything goes. There are bad hunches as well as good ones. Moreover, what has been unorthodox may rapidly become the new common sense; it may become the rigidly orthodox, something not to be questioned. But we have to be aware of our over-attachment to common sense, to the familiar, to the safety of staying within our old habits and our 'home' territory.

When my Indian nephew, now a successful entrepreneur in his mid-forties, was fifteen or so, he had an idea that he confidently and excitedly told me. Why not have a cricketing competition, he said, not between states in India, not over four days or even one, but much shorter and between cities? Would not this excite people? Would it not make money? I'm sorry to say that I discouraged him. Shorter than 50 overs a side? And what's so special about city teams? And what's more, what can he tell me about cricket? My response, though superficially polite, no doubt conveyed that I thought he should come back when he knew a bit more.

How wrong I was! Two decades later, more or less exactly what he was proposing became, with a few embellishments, the Indian Premier League, one of the most successful sporting ventures ever, engaging the imaginations of millions of new followers of the game, and later exported to most other cricket-playing countries (with the variant 'Hundred' competition due to start in England in 2020, though because of the pandemic, postponed to 2021).

* * *

One quality that might justifiably have been mentioned in the Preamble is generosity; first, generosity of mind, which encourages ideas from all quarters. Second, and equally important, is generosity of spirit through action. When Trevor Bayliss finished his stint as coach of the England team, he said that he found it incredible that Australian players were 'invited over to play county cricket [i.e. first-class cricket in England] ahead of an Ashes series'. He wanted the ECB to 'have a look at that' – that is, to put a stop to it.

I prefer an alternative approach. In 1987, India played Pakistan in a Test series in India. The first four matches were drawn. The last, at Bangalore, was played on a spinners' pitch. India needed 221 to win. With the match poised on the rest day (India were precariously placed on 95–4), Bishan Bedi, the legendary Indian slow left-arm bowler, then retired, happened to meet Pakistan's spinners, Iqbal Qasim and Tauseef Ahmed, at a social event. Bishan told them that he thought his own protégé, Maninder Singh, who had taken 7 wickets for 27 runs in the first innings of the match, had been trying too hard on this turning pitch in the second innings. He implied that the primary requirement was to put the ball in the right place, letting the pitch do the work, rather than trying to impart a lot of spin. Qasim later said that this advice helped Pakistan win the match – by a mere 16 runs. When this became public knowledge, some Indian fans were angry with Bedi for what they saw as his disloyalty, though what he said on this occasion was not exactly rocket science. In the 1930s, Australia's 'Chuck' Fleetwood-Smith is said, similarly, to have shared the secret of a special grip with his Ashes opponent Hedley Verity. When criticised for giving help to the opposition, he is said to have replied: 'Art is universal.'

I side with Fleetwood-Smith. The generosity behind a sense of universal art trumps the protectiveness and meanness of tribal rivalry.

13

FROM BEYOND THE BOUNDARY

'Modern culture is so much about the moment, everything
consumed and thrown away, everything "got up to be exciting",
and we struggle to retain a proper sense of perspective, an
understanding that we are here for just a short while and that
we have a duty to look after our world for future generations.'

Stephen Chalke

Soon after I started to write this book, Anthony Wreford, then
president of the MCC and the person responsible for inviting me to
give the Spirit of Cricket Lecture in May 2019 that started this ball
rolling, made a suggestion: how about inviting a range of 'cricket
people' to respond to a survey about how they see the spirit of cricket
developing in the future; and giving a chapter to their views in
the book? (Apart from other advantages, it would, I thought, be a
welcome relief to the reader, to hear other voices.)

With these questions in mind, I followed Wreford's suggestion.
I asked the following questions of an assorted group of 'cricket people'.

> *How do you think the ethics of the game is*
> *changing and will change?*
>
> *As everyone plays more and more short and very*
> *short forms of the game, are we at a crossroads?*

Will the phrase 'It's not cricket' make any sense in the future?

Would you be willing to let me know how you think things are changing or will change? I'm not very good at predicting, myself!

Several restricted their comments to the past and present, apparently ignoring the future, but often with implications for what might be expected, given current trends. Many focused on international cricket – but of course there are also wider worries about attitudes and behaviour across the culture of the whole game.

Here, I present much of what they wrote. Except for organising responses under different headings, I've kept myself out of this chapter.

1. SHIFTING STANDARDS

Suresh Menon (cricket writer and editor)

We pour into sport our greatest passions because we think that is a way of rescuing it from its essential meaninglessness and transforming it into something real. So why should cricket answer to a higher morality – the spirit of the game?

The answer lies in its artificiality. Cricket cannot be a mere reflection of society but must aspire to a superior realm. It is fantasy, and in a fantasy world we should aim for perfection, for the ideal. The process is important even if it is often observed only in the breach.

We inject cricket with a greater moral purpose than, say, business or politics. Even politicians who have moral issues are expected to be honest on the sports field. Bill Clinton might have cheated on his wife, but had he cheated on a golf course, there would have been no redemption.

That we had to tag on a Preamble to the Laws about the Spirit of the Game probably means we had lost track of this important aspect of the game. Cricket reveals character. A touch of ambiguity between what is within the laws and what falls on the side of 'spirit' is a wonderful test of a player's integrity.

Mike Atherton (ex-cricketer and commentator)

One man's spirit of cricket is far removed from another's. As the game spreads – Afghanistan, Nepal, Papua New Guinea, America, etc. – local customs will alter what has been traditionally accepted as the spirit of cricket, rendering it utterly changed from its original conception to the point where it becomes almost meaningless.

Stephen Chalke (former club cricketer and writer)

As a generalisation I would say that in my lifetime the spirit of cricket has weakened significantly, among all social classes and at all levels, but that it does still exist.

You would be surprised by some of the situations that occur in the lower leagues. One team turned up with ten men. They persuaded the girlfriend of a team member to stick on some pads and go in at number eleven. She stayed in long enough for the total to increase by three runs. The opposition were furious, even more furious when she didn't come out to field, and most furious of all when they lost by one run.

On another occasion, when I was captaining a club third eleven, we went to play another club's fourth eleven. Their captain explained that as they had twelve he was standing down . . . In came number three. He played immaculate forward defensive shots to my first two balls, and it was immediately clear that he was not a fourth-teamer. He admitted that their first-eleven game had been cancelled; he came to watch, so their captain was lying when he said that they were one short . . . I later learned that the number three was captain of Wiltshire.

The [Wiltshire] League introduced regulations to prevent unsporting attitudes. I remember thinking: 'Wouldn't it be better if we appealed to the spirit of the game?', but I knew, in this modern age of win-if-you-can cynicism, that I was being naive. The offending captain was sitting next to me at the meeting. He leaned across to me to say, as if in justification: 'We did it with you because we were trying to win promotion.'

Every year at those League AGMs we were discussing some such incident from the summer, and every time the answer was a fresh regulation. The print in the handbook got smaller and smaller to accommodate all the extra regulations. More often than not, clubs faced with all this small print looked to find fresh dodges rather than refer to the spirit behind them.

Rodney Marsh (ex-cricketer)

I've never thought much about the spirit of cricket but always believed cricket was a game to be played hard but fair. Just what is hard and what is fair may well be intertwined with the true spirit of the game.

The captain has had and will always have a great influence on the behaviour of his team. This should never be changed. What should be changed however is the team being told by coaches or even administrators to make sure they make a lot of noise in the field to put pressure on the batsmen. What puts pressure on the two batsmen is really good bowling and fielding.

John Inverarity (ex-cricketer, ex-head teacher)

I cannot abide –

* Yapping: 'Well bowled. Got 'im worried, etc.' It's juvenile and pathetic! When I umpired at schools, I jumped on it and would not tolerate it.

* Sledging: Anything premeditated and designed to put a player off his game. It is understood that racial abuse and sexual preference harassment are not permitted. Then why on earth are other forms of harassment permitted? Ian Chappell says the umpires should stop it. I think there should not be a need for umpires to stop it. It comes back to the players, and if not the players, then the captains. Then, if not the players and captains, the umpires. Perhaps it goes even further, to the way fathers and mothers raise their children, teaching them to behave respectfully and decently.

* Time-wasting: Late in a Test match, the team that is trying to reduce the damage often wastes time blatantly. It is demeaning for the captain to resort to this. Where is his honour?

* Poor walking to and, especially, from the crease: What are batsmen attempting to convey when they are dismissed and saunter off holding the bat halfway down the blade? Are they attempting to demean the bowler on the occasion of their dismissal? I would very much like somebody to articulate cleverly what this is attempting to convey. Could you? Perhaps Clive James could have done so, brilliantly, but now it is too late for that. (A wonderful intellect and turn of phrase.)

Ted Dexter (ex-cricketer)

Any form of sledging should be penalised. Penalties to include the bowler being taken off and a time interval before he can bowl again. Also a points system against the captain, leading to suspension.

Isabelle Duncan (ex-player and commentator)
Increasing camera angles glued to a player's every move make it much harder for some types of cheating on the field of play – scuffing up the pitch or ball-tampering are obvious examples.

2. MOVES TOWARDS THE MEASURABLE

Stephen Chalke
My work as an oral historian has mostly been with cricketers who played in the first quarter-century after the war, so a lot of my way of seeing the issue is shaped by those men. I think that, for quite a while afterwards, the war shaped our collective attitude towards right and wrong. Tom Cartwright puts it well: 'The war was still so close. People could see the consequences of doing wrong.' Lancashire batsman Geoff Edrich, a prisoner of the Japanese, said 'what's the good of winning if you cheat?'

In cricket as in society, we have dismantled (to a considerable degree) an old class system, based on birth and education, and replaced it with one based on money and achievement. Much of that change is for the better, but it has led to a decline in a sense of community and to a greater sense of striving to better oneself. This is reflected in sport where considerations of fair play have become secondary to the importance of winning. [Ex-wicketkeeper] Keith [Andrew] – [a master of his craft, who went about his business with quiet assurance] – was passionate about upholding the spirit of cricket. 'Cricket is a game,' he said. 'You play to win. But that's not why you play cricket.'

In cricket there has been the added factor that, to keep pace with a faster-moving way of life, we have developed shorter and shorter versions of the game. Inevitably this tilts the balance further towards winning being the be-all and end-all of the activity.

Further, there has been a decline in religion, at least among the Christian part of our population, and I think that also weakens our sense of shared values.

John Major (former prime minister; cricket-lover and writer)
We live today in a climate in which nothing is unchallenged, nor seen to be unchallengeable. Politics has changed – in many countries –in ways that are distinctively negative. Democracy is in retreat while autocracy rises.

The point is simple: traditional mores – the spirit of cricket, the accepted traditions of politics – are no longer sacrosanct, and change can be both dramatic and swift. Little thought or planning seems to be given to either the long-term, or to the secondary effects of change. When primacy is given to immediacy, decision-making is skewed to the short term, which merely defers problems.

Cricket is an old game that rose to prominence as a recreation with little opposition: today, it faces huge competition . . . In an age demanding swift outcomes, Test and County cricket is therefore at a disadvantage. It may be that Club cricket is too: some clubs (not least in the Lancashire League) appear keen to restrict the game to its T20 format because that fits in more easily with family commitments. It is becoming clear that five-day Test matches are at risk, as near-empty grounds reveal, outside of England or Australia.

Ian Rickson (theatre director)
I'm interested in how much 'the spirit of cricket' is an ambiguous term. It is freighted with empire as well as fairness. It has a patrician quality as well as other more complex qualities.

We have 'pay to view' formats that monetise the game in an extraordinary way, and at least in the UK make it an elite sport: you can only watch it if you can afford Sky Sports, and only play it – mostly – if you go to private school. We invest less and less in school sports, with the result that many education establishments sell off their sports fields and teachers are so pressured they can't find time to coach kids after school.

Mike Procter (ex-player and match referee)
So much money I suppose leads towards playing strictly by the book (i.e. by the laws), as opposed to by the spirit of the game.

3. CORRUPTION

Isabelle Duncan
Perhaps the biggest threat of all to the integrity of the game is match-fixing. It is a thorn in the side of world cricket as criminal gangs make millions out of bribing and coercing players to guarantee certain outcomes. Here, the 'Spirit of Cricket' must stand tall and play a very public and active role in fighting this evil. If the ICC are serious about anti-corruption, there is an opportunity for those advocating the spirit of cricket to work in partnership with them and make its presence felt.

Mike Procter
Corruption must be stamped out at all costs. This requires player education but sometimes, human nature being what it is, it falls on deaf ears. As match referee at T20 matches, corruption happens. There is a worry that this could get to women's cricket.

I could tell you stories. But one problem is that exposure produces stigma. We reported one player to his board and they did nothing as it was a T20 tournament. He was picked the following week for his country.

There is a Catch-22 situation: do you highlight and so give sport a bad name? Or keep quiet? But it is definitely out there more than you realise.

4. PURPOSES BEHIND THE LAWS

Anthony Wreford (cricketer and administrator)

My assumption is that technology gets better and continues to provide a greater degree of accuracy on decisions . . . so that cricket decisions will be more black-and-white as technology will have removed most of the grey areas where individuals currently make their own call (mainly in claiming catches and walking). My other assumption is that other grey areas (e.g. Mankading) will ultimately be cut out, as the laws of the game will continue to tackle ambiguous situations.

I don't know if you have come across the expression 'Purpose', which is frequently used by younger people in the context of a business or organisation? It's become a fashionable expression as companies and individuals examine what lies at the heart of a particular entity. For example, businesses in financial services are doing a lot to try to demonstrate how they can help people invest in companies with a social conscience, an environmental strategy etc. I think you can adapt 'purpose' to a cricket team where other qualities and characteristics may be added to the overall desire to win. 'Purpose' could include, for instance, being entertaining, winning with a smile, being respected, playing fairly, no sledging etc.

5. PERSONAL RELATIONSHIPS AND CURRENT MORES

John Major

Modern cricket is not especially culpable: not walking, claiming a false catch: player betting on games: match-fixing – are all nearly as old as the game itself. In a small minority of top-class games, one detects some misbehaviour. However, at the 'grass roots', such misconduct is no more prevalent than it was in the past, indeed probably less so.

On a wider canvas, the role of women in sport – in life generally – has changed dramatically, which was necessary and welcome.

Vic Marks (ex-player and writer)
I've always been a bit sceptical about the good old days when the spirit of cricket was supposed to be so prevalent. I fancy there have been a lot of double standards. From W. G. onwards, I guess. Leaving aside bodyline, when 'only one team is playing cricket out there', there's Bradman claiming the catch against Wally Hammond at the start of the 1946/7 tour (perhaps he did indeed catch it, who knows?); there's Cowdrey who seemed to walk but only when it suited him; there's the Aussies being demonised in the Chappell era yet dear old Rodney [Marsh] calling back Arkle [Derek Randall] in the Centenary Test etc. Is modern-day ball-tampering any different from the seam-picking that meant that the ball almost shredded your fingers when catching it in the '60s, '70s and '80s?

If anything, I think the spirit of cricket might relate to the respect/friendship generated among those playing the game as team-mates and opponents. There is often a bond, isn't there? Perhaps this was more evident in years gone by, when there may have been less vicious, calculated sledging. Probably more time was spent with opponents then, so it was easier to respect them and build friendships. Rival wicketkeepers would huddle in corners and one presumes they were talking about the differing qualities of various makes of inner gloves.

Players don't do that so much now, I guess, but I still see plenty of signs of mutual respect. This may well stem from the fact that the best players are often thrown together in IPL or other domestic T20 league sides around the world; they get to know one another, recognise qualities and share experiences – and away we go. There is not so much time to do that in the T20 era, but it's clearly still possible. For example, I notice that Faf du Plessis speaks of Ben Stokes with awe and affection (they were once IPL team-mates). So I think the game still brings people together.

Isabelle Duncan

The laws and technology (sometimes inadvertently) do their best to protect the spirit of the game, but much must rest in the laps of the players themselves. The old adages 'be gracious in defeat and humble in victory' and 'always respect your team, opponents and the authority of the umpires' are universal and stand the test of time. Without decent human behaviour and good old-fashioned manners, cricket is in danger of spiralling to the depths of loutish football and becoming unrecognisable.

Simon Taufel (ex-international umpire)

For me, I was taught how to play the game by older people such as my captains and club mentors. Going forward, sadly, these people are fewer in number. A lot of new players, including kids, are not being inducted in the game, its meaning, its traditions and how we play. I wonder if we should have something to replace the system I grew up with? If so, what document/text or videos could be produced to refer them to?

Captains used to be the ones to control the behaviour of their teams – now we have the Code of Conduct and administrators to deal with that. I wonder what the spirit of the game will look like fifty years from now.

Sport has the opportunity to buck the trend of the deteriorating values and behaviours in society as character is more important than a cover drive.

Mike Procter

I always felt that part of the job of match referee was trying to get teams to play in the right spirit and respect each other. Before each day's play, I would speak to coaches or captains . . . asking if there were any problems etc. Both teams must be playing to the same set of rules, but beyond that, within a broadly shared 'spirit of the game' . . .

Culminating in the disgraceful behaviour of Australia in South Africa [in 2018], the game was certainly getting very ugly. New Zealand again showed the cricket world how it ought to be done and what a breath of fresh air they were!

[But] the general attitude around the cricket world does look healthy.

6. VIGILANCE AND HOPE

Stephen Chalke

How will it evolve in future years? It will almost certainly need constant policing, much more than it once did, and it will need the sport's leadership to be strong and to care for the game beyond the financial balance sheet and the winning and losing. There is an irony – albeit a welcome one – in MCC becoming such a force for the good in all this.

The danger in relying on policing, rather than on commonly held values, can be seen in football, where players factor into their behaviour a calculation about whether it pays to commit a foul. 'I stop a goal being scored and, if I get sent off at this stage of the game, it will probably be worth it.' They call it 'taking one for the team' where once we would have called it cheating.

Our nation is still riven by Brexit, and I do fear for the future. The agenda of many of those at the heart of the Brexit project was to create a low-tax, low-regulation economy, and I see that as accelerating the intense commercialisation – the Americanisation, if you like – of our culture. If we do go down that road, then the values underpinning the Spirit of Cricket will become harder to maintain.

Ian Rickson

For my part – like Harold [Pinter] – I love the game, I love its similarities to theatre, its strange mixture of grace and savagery. But I lament how wonderful moments – like [Ben] Stokes's innings in the Headingley Test – have largely been priced out of the public's grasp. Cricket, along with its spirit, is in danger of becoming a strangely elitist sport like 'real' tennis or croquet.

So, to sum up, I'm perhaps saying 'the spirit of cricket' has gone from a colonial maxim, to teach subjects to obey a system of rules, to a global market run by billionaires (Murdoch and whoever owns the IPL). Yet it goes on.

And we love it.

14

GOLDEN CALVES' FOOT JELLY

'[Magna Carta] was not a peace accord botched up to meet a sudden crisis . . . It had a quality of inherent strength because it expressed the will of the people, or at any rate the articulate representatives of the people.'

Tom Bingham

Like other forms of life, cricket is the outcome of informal social contract. It is a practice held together and supported by a set of mostly tacit agreements, all part of our legacy from past generations. Entering the world of cricket is to enter such traditions and expectations, and (hopefully) feel safe enough within them, just as from the beginning of life we are held by the whole gamut of care, love and values offered by our parents and our culture. We stand on the shoulders both of our forerunners and of the general culture. It is from this basis that we argue for reformation and change. I suggest that this underlying internalised agreement is the most important element in the spirit of cricket, more important than any maxims or edicts pronounced from above.

Bingham's quote implies that there is a wisdom in crowds as well as the potential for cruelty and barbarism. And there are many voices and attitudes within the crowd.

The spirit of cricket empowers the game from grass roots up. My father believed the game should be played 'properly'. He *minded* about bowlers bowling deliberately wide to him. The spirit of the game is part of what makes it matter to players and followers. It is part of what gives it purpose, meaning and emphasis.

Arthur Wellard, the old Somerset and England cricketer, who later played for Harold Pinter's 'Gaieties' team until he was seventy-three years old, and then took up umpiring, was a demanding mentor and critic. Pinter describes playing a beautiful cover drive in a game at Eastbourne, 'probably the best shot I ever played in my life. A few overs later I was clean bowled. Arthur was waiting for me in front of the pavilion. What do you think you're doing? he asked . . . playing back to a pitched-up ball? . . . Oh, I said. Well anyway, what did you think of that cover drive? Never mind the cover drive, Arthur said. Just stop playing back to full-length balls . . . Sorry, Arthur, I said.'

Pinter loved that no-nonsense attitude, Wellard's respect for mastery of the basics of the craft, his prioritising this over a flash of brilliance. On another occasion, Pinter got his head down, staying at the wicket for an hour and a quarter for some twenty-five runs, warding off disaster. On his return, Arthur 'looked at me steadily and said "I was proud of you"'. Pinter comments: 'I don't suppose any words said to me have given me greater pleasure.'

The Preamble to the Laws of Cricket is more an articulation by representatives of the cricketing world than a proclamation *de haut en bas* – from high to low.

There are times when cricket, like life, produces a fine exemplar, someone who nudges, even perhaps inspires, many of us to remember what is foundational to its spirit, to recall deep-seated values that are at times overridden by baser drives such as petulance, tribalism, self-righteousness, arrogance or triumphalism, and jolts or guides us into a better way of being. I'm thinking again of Brendon McCullum, who renewed not only his own basic love of the game, but also influenced others, in his own team and beyond, to re-connect with theirs for themselves.

It sounds pretentious to compare him to the great moral figures of our time – Nelson Mandela or Mahatma Gandhi – but the comparison has its point: in cricket and sport as in life in general we learn from those who, by giving voice and action to our better selves, both confirm and enhance them. Through them, values crystallise anew. Jesus said: 'I come not to destroy the law but to fulfil it' – that is, to give it its fuller meaning and scope.

The expression of this kind of spirit is to be seen in action; but also in a person's disposition and open-mindedness. David Sheppard opposed apartheid, especially as it appeared in cricket, over several decades. Later it was his spirit of fairness that led him to disappoint some anti-apartheid campaigners by accepting the invitation of the chairman of the South African Cricket Board, Ali Bacher, to see for himself the progress that had been made since 1968 in fostering cricket in the townships. Joe Root and Virat Kohli showed their underlying spirit in the spontaneous way their courage was expressed.

Many of our tendencies are generous. We all (or almost all) know there is something better and more truthful in how we generally go about things than what our occasional descents into dishonesty, thoughtlessness or rancour suggest. The spirit of cricket – like 'truth' or 'goodness' or 'the rule of law' – alludes to an ideal, an aspiration, but it also recognises a reality. We all have an inclination towards the good, however much we fall short. We might say that it's in our nature; I like the term 'second nature', which acknowledges the impact of early conditioning and development without denying the idea of a basic inheritance.

We are imbued with a sense of fairness. Even Machiavelli, arguing that, in order not to be taken advantage of, leaders must eschew humanity, mercy, honesty and justice, thereby acknowledges the appeal of these virtues.

The spirit of cricket is inclusive, emphasising that cricket offers everyone a level playing field. Like the rule of law, it is essentially democratic. No one is above it, or below it.

* * *

Jonathan Biss, the American pianist, when asked if he had learned a lot about Beethoven-the-person from recording all his thirty-two piano sonatas, said he had learned about his intensity, but also his humanity; in such a turbulent person there is a great deal of love, even tenderness. But, Biss added, he had learned more about the world, and about himself. He feels *he* is a better person for it. There is nothing like Beethoven for making one more empathetic.

Would I, would you, have been less of a person, including being less empathic, without cricket? Does the spirit of cricket as expressed today nudge us, and society at large, in good directions? Or has it, the game, 'lost its soul'?

There have always been doom-laden predictions for cricket, like Rowland Bowen's: 'This is no trough into which the game has fallen: it is a decline into the grave'.

David Underdown, comparing late twentieth-century England's focus on money and markets with late eighteenth-century England, when there was a loss of local community spirit as money became a more potent, corrupting influence, questions whether in each case cricket 'lost its soul', and had a negative impact on the broader culture. He writes: 'The subordination of the Hambledon Cricket Club to the needs of its aristocratic patrons both reflected and contributed to the decay of one part of rural England Is it totally fanciful to suggest that the subordination of modern cricket to the interests of its private sponsors may have an equally profound impact on our culture?'

So: has the game lost something vital? Has playing for fun become secondary to winning at all costs? Does he who pays the piper call the entire tune? And is the game as a result less positive in its impact on those who play it, and thus more damaging to the general culture?

Underdown may be right about the eighteenth century, but I think the parallels with our own situation are exaggerated. There are indeed risks; society inevitably colours sport, and sport makes its own contribution to the broader society. Every generation idealises what went (or what was alleged to have gone) before. Every generation has to be vigilant against its own prejudices and assumptions. Every set of values has inbuilt risks. We do indeed swing between expectations that are too high-minded, and the opposite tendency to believe or act as though anything goes.

But positive influences and values persist. Cricketers still play for love of the game, at all levels. They still, largely, aim at the spirit of the game, at playing 'hard but fair'. And fair play is a matter of inner integration and integrity. As with Sheppard, Root and Kohli, character is more important than simply following rules. It is a matter of the kind of person we have become, not only in our actions but in our dispositions. Our personal inner values inform our actions, and general values inform our laws.

One theme running through this book has been that spirit is deeper than law, general attitude more ramifying and influential than behavioural decency and obedience. We need good laws in cricket and beyond, and they need to be imbued with values. But laws can't cover everything.

Surveillance threatens this freedom. In Albanian novelist Ismail Kadare's *The Palace of Dreams*, dreams are collected from all over the empire, to be examined for seditious content by bureaucrats in the 'palace'. The aim is to nip opposition in the bud, before it blooms in action. Today there are apprehensions about neuroscience; in an unspecified future, perhaps even now, could it pry into our *'forum internum'* – our inner personal space – and even lead to persecution? And might our own or foreign governments manipulate our voting by gaining access to our prejudices and values without our assent?

Law rightly takes account of *'mens rea'*, or guilty mind, but only if it motivates and thus characterises actions. In cricket for example, umpires have to decide whether a collision between batsman and bowler was an accident or the outcome of deliberate obstruction by either party. In the broader sphere of life, the man who buys chemicals to make bombs, stores them in his attic, communicates with others about occasions on which the bombs might do maximum damage to those identified by the group as enemies – all this may establish a conspiracy to terrorist activity, and be rightly chargeable and punishable by law. In such a case, the mindset of terrorism has entered into the public arena. It may be difficult to differentiate between intention and mere fantasy, but they are different.

* * *

We have seen that some are reluctant to use terms like 'spirit' or 'soul'. I wonder if their objections are partly, and in some cases, metaphysical – if, that is, the unease is to do with the noun ('spirit'), which may seem to refer to a transcendent 'thing', to be contrasted with things of a material kind? 'Spirit', like 'soul', has often been used in religious contexts to refer to an immortal and immaterial essence that survives death. To some this may feel like the hazy entity, the will-o'-the-wisp hovering above the pavilion at Lord's cricket ground.

In their ordinary contemporary use, however, these words need not have any such ontological implications. It's true that the spirit of cricket alludes to more than mere behaviour. It refers to orientation, disposition and passion. It accommodates humour and pain, generosity and meanness. Perhaps not quite with Beethoven's range, it can either enlarge our capacity for empathy or reduce us to cynicism and to treating others as mere ciphers without inner worlds.

We vary in how much our nature makes us prone more to negative or positive shifts, in how much we struggle with our own tendencies and try to get to an honest appraisal of ourselves and the world. Some are suspicious to the level of paranoia, others are trusting to the point of naivety. Such mindsets constitute the spirit we display or indeed try to hide. They frame our behaviour, organising it and limiting it in largely automatic ways.

Mindsets are as real as outer behaviour, which they guide and inhabit. Along with our actions and our reflections, they make us what we are.

When we feel threatened, anxious, humiliated, deprived, our hold on ordinarily civilised behaviour is destabilised, especially if the trauma is cumulative and prolonged. We are liable to tip over into panic, despair or cynicism. We lose our ethical bearings, and often our own resilience. ('I'm a failure. Why live?') We lose empathy. We become aggressive, fighting to push people out of our way, even cruel. This happens individually and collectively. At such times civilised behaviour and attitudes come to look like a veneer, a thin, fragile covering for something more raw, more desperate and more fundamental.

Idealisation is one root of this. If our values are unrealistically high, if we romanticise cricket too much, if we build structures in the air, will-o'-the-wisps above the pavilion at Lord's, a puff of wind may dispel them and they plummet to the ground. As with marriage, we need to enter it with high hopes and passion, yet we have to learn over time that its success depends as much on struggle and tolerance. Our hopes should be high, but not too high.

Biss recommends a 1962 recording by Rudolf Serkin of the 'Moonlight' Sonata. He particularly admired the 'integrity' of his playing. Serkin does not, Biss suggests, set out to make it beautiful; instead he gets the 'life and death quality of the music, its intensity'.

He hints at a broader truth here. Aim at beauty and you tend to get sentimentality; aim at happiness and end up with mania or schmaltz; at purity and end with parsimony; at plenitude and you arrive at 'anything goes'. In cricket, if you ignore and in your conscious life dispel your more earthy emotions, if your target is too lofty, you float up to the cloud. Or your cloud collapses, into cynicism and despair or into dullness and platitude.

Journalist and broadcaster Alan Gibson wrote in 1976 about the need for a psychological hinterland that resists such tendencies:

> I believe that nearly all the writers on sport have had interests in other fields, and consequently a sense of proportion. Hazlitt, [Bernard] Darwin, Cardus, Arlott are names which come quickly to mind . . . It would never occur to these men to make a golden calf of sport: but a golden calf it has become, in our society, with thousands of businessmen and television and radio producers, quite apart from the journalists, fighting for their spoonful of golden calves' foot jelly.

It's wrong to think that the fragility of resilience, the fact that we all have our tipping points, and that in our middle-of-the-night crises we lose our sense of solidarity, means that the *real self* is selfish and raw, that a good spirit is a mere figment, an illusion, a gloss that conceals reality. Crises may tip us in opposite directions. Though the coronavirus pandemic has given rise to selfishness and denial, it has also prompted selflessness, community spirit, a widening of the notion of 'we'. We pull together. We expand simpler and cruder affiliations for the common good, for which many make sacrifices. Some become truly heroic. Danger brings out the best as well as the worst in us. Whether we consider society at large, or small-scale activities within society, like cricket, it is impossible to know which way we will turn.

But we have a better chance of moving towards social cohesion and mutual support, towards a spirit of cooperation, if we acknowledge the whole, mixed self. As D. H. Lawrence writes:

> Plato makes the perfect ideal being tremble in me. But that's only a bit of me . . . The Ten Commandments set the old Adam shivering in me, warning me that I am a thief and a murderer, unless I

watch it. But even the old Adam is only a bit of me . . . We should ask for no absolutes, or absolute. Once and for all and for ever, let us have done with the ugly imperialism of any absolute. There is no absolute good, there is nothing absolutely right. The whole is a strange assembly of apparently incongruous parts, slipping past one another . . . In all this change, I maintain a certain integrity. But woe betide me if I try to put my finger on it. If I say of myself, I am this, I am that! – then, if I stick to it, I turn into a stupid fixed thing like a lamp-post. I shall never know wherein lies my integrity, my individuality, my me. I can never know it . . . In life, there is right and wrong, good and bad, all the time. But what is right in one case is wrong in another. Right and wrong is an instinct: but an instinct of the whole consciousness in a man, bodily, mental, spiritual at once. For out of the full play of all things emerges the only thing that is anything, the wholeness of a man, the wholeness of a woman, man alive, and live woman.

There is no absolute 'real self', no fundamental spirit or lack of it. We are neither all nature nor all nurture. We lie somewhere on a spectrum, from baseness to generosity and grace. And we fluctuate.

So my suggestion is: let's expect a lot, but not too much. Let's avoid the 'ugly imperialism of any absolute', and be suspicious of our rose-tinted glasses. Don't hype cricket up into something elevated, a golden calf, or imagine that it is *too* special. If we do, we risk being left with nothing (the grave), or with something flat and boring, dull as ditchwater: a drab list of solemn platitudes.

And yet, and yet. Cricket *is* special, and our better selves can prevail.

POSTSCRIPT:

THE PREAMBLE

The wording of the Preamble came on the scene only recently, in 2000. Like Magna Carta it was articulated by representatives of the people, putting into written form what had been held to be of value through (largely) shared values and communal action.

I too think it valuable, sitting there as a preface to, a context for, the Laws, reminding us of the game's broad context, highlighting the informal contract that underlies the necessity for laws that express values such as positivity, safety, balance and equality. The Preamble also reminds us that laws can't cover everything.

In speaking about cricket's spirit there is always a risk of piety and smugness. We easily assume that *we* have it and *they* don't. We blithely believe that cricket is morally superior to other games. We sermonise, speaking the speak but not walking the walk.

But despite these risks, we do look to cricket for qualities such as generosity, courtesy, and respect for the laws and for the officials who interpret them. I am at least tempted by the belief that we cricket lovers have some special hopes and expectations for the way cricket is to be, and often is, played and promoted.

Nevertheless, the official Preamble veers away from the punchiness of maxim. 'Do as you would be done by.' Such brevity leaves a lot to the recipient. It does not patronise or preach. It reminds me of Gertrude Stein's last words on her deathbed. She asked the question: 'What is the answer?' When no answer was forthcoming, she asked another: 'In that case, what is the question?' She then died.

So if, as I believe, there should be a Preamble to the Laws of Cricket, how much should it include? Should it spell out a wide range of potential failings in relation to fair play and to the spirit of the game? Should it explicitly address not only players but all those who might be accused of lacking it?

Rightly, in my opinion, the draughtsmen/women of the 2017 version succeeded in considerably reducing the length of the Preamble, to 163 words from the 417 of the 2000 Preamble.

My own view is: the shorter the better. Less is more.

Here is a version of the Preamble that I'd prefer:

> All those involved in cricket should respect the integrity of the game. On the field and off it, the spirit of cricket asks us to 'play hard but fair'. And let's not lose the essence of the word 'play'!

Only thirty-nine words!

And you, dear patient Reader? Where do you stand?

Shaun Botterill/Getty Images

ACKNOWLEDGEMENTS

Writing the book took rather longer than a year; but it emerges from a lifetime of argument, debate and discussion. Some acknowledgements appear or are implied in the text, through references to books and people. But it is hard to give credit and thanks to the many people who over the decades have influenced my mature, or at any rate my elderly, views.

Perhaps my greatest debt goes to my father, Horace, who died in 2007, for introducing me to this form of life; and to my mother and sisters, who were even occasionally allowed to field, for tolerating and supporting it and me. Also to my current family, comprising my wife Mana, our children Mischa and Lara, and their delightful families.

The book would not have been written without Anthony Wreford, president of MCC in 2018–19, and the MCC Committee, who invited me to give the Cowdrey Lecture on the Spirit of Cricket in 2019, and have offered much, both before and since. I'm grateful too to members of the MCC World Cricket Committee, in particular to John Stephenson and Fraser Stewart, for rich discussions on many of the issues over many years. Janet Fisher and Debbie Moore (both at Lord's) have always given generously of their time.

Probably it would not have been written without the suggestion, made immediately following my lecture, by my publisher and editor Andreas Campomar and agent Matthew Hamilton, of a book on this topic. I think they were afraid I might be insisting on an unsellable and probably unwritable (by me) book on the death instinct.

I would like to thank very particularly Alan Budd, Stephen Chalke, David Kynaston and Mana – all of whom have read whole drafts, and introduced me to new ideas and to books I was not even aware of and have corrected errors. They have helped me make my thoughts clearer on many different issues. They have all shown the spirit of (as David put it) the 'republic of letters' in their generosity – not so different from the spirit of cricket!

Hugh Brody, Suresh Menon, Kannan Navaratnem, Matthew Hamilton, Mischa Gorchov Brearley and David Millar have read and responded insightfully and encouragingly to chunks of my writings. Nigel Peters and Peter Leaver helped me greatly with the law and its letter, and Nigel also for much of the detail of the 'Monkeygate' issue. Russell Cake was very helpful on the Laws of cricket.

Similarly, I have had conversations and email discussion, recently and over the years, with many others, including Ram Guha, Mike Procter, Rod Marsh, John Inverarity, Ed Smith, Vintcent van der Bijl, John Major, Mervyn King, Mike Atherton, Mike Gatting and Vic Marks.

I'd like to thank all my 'cricket people' correspondents in Chapter 13.

Many, too many to mention, and invidious to those whose names don't jump to my mind, have influenced my thinking and given me important leads and pieces of information. Among them I will mention: Diana Bass, Scyld Berry, Victor Blank, David Bloomfield, Ian Botham, Geoff Boycott, Gaby Braun, Derek Brewer, David Burston, Chris Butcher, Roland Butcher, Tom Cartwright, Greg Chappell, Ian Chappell, Fakhry Davids, Rahul Dravid, Fae Dussart, John Emburey, Kate Fitzpatrick, Keith Fletcher, Andy Flower, Angus Fraser,

Charles Fry, Jacobo Quintanilla Gomez, Graham Gooch, Michael Holding, Richard Hutton, Clive Hitchcock, Raymond Illingworth, Leon Kleimberg, John Lever, Tony Lewis, Dennis Lillee, Hilary Mantel, Robin Marlar, Sam Mendes, Geoff Miller, Deryck Murray, Irma Brenman Pick, Daniel Pick, Bob Platt, Clive Radley, David Richardson, Ian Rickson, Juliet Rosenfeld, Kumar Sangakkara, Clem Seecharan, Mike Selvey, Andrew Strauss, Robin Sen Gupta, Margot Waddell, Simon Wilde, Rowan Williams, Bob Willis, Shaan Zaveri.

My editor, who fights an ongoing battle with me over my tendency to be too academic, has resisted Notes, Bibliography and References for this book. As a result, I don't know how to refer to articles and books (and their authors) that have been invaluable for the project. The authors include R.S. Rait Kerr, Rowland Bowen, Jonathan Rosen, C. Cowden Clarke, Colin Cowdrey, David Underdown, C.L.R. James, Vintcent van der Bijl, Tom Bingham, Amartya Sen, Stephen Chalke, Stephen Fay, David Kynaston, Geoff Lemon, Scyld Berry, Simon Wilde, Adrian Stokes, Ramachandra Guha, Suresh Menon, Jonathan Sacks, Ronald Heifetz, Mathew Syed, Rowan Williams, Steve Waugh, Lynn Layton, W.E.B. du Bois, Fakhry Davids, Jonathan Lear, Donald Moss, James Kerr, Iris Murdoch, John Wisdom, Ludwig Wittgenstein, Johan Huizinga, Wilfred Bion, Marion Milner, D. H. Lawrence and Alan Gibson.

As with my previous two books, Little, Brown, in particular Jo Wickham, have been caring and efficient; as has Matthew Hamilton.

Andreas Campomar has been omnipresent. I would say it is *our* book. Andreas is a great facilitator, who manages to get thoughts going and flowing without losing sight of the equally important editorial quality, that of putting a stop to them before they flood the whole field.

Thank you.

INDEX